Advent to Epiphany

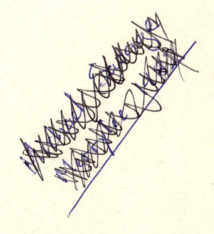

Acknowledgment is made to Penguin Books Ltd, for a quotation from *The Shaking of The Foundations;* Editions du Cerf for a quotation from *La Minifestation du Seigneur;* and for quotations from the *Revised Standard Version Common Bible*, copyrighted © 1973

Vincent Ryan

Advent to Epiphany

Veritas Publications Dublin 1977

First published 1977 by
Veritas Publications,
7-8 Lower Abbey Street, Dublin 1.

©1977 Vincent Ryan

Set in 11/12 Baskerville.
Origination by Joe Healy Typesetting, Dublin.
Printed and bound in the
Republic of Ireland by
Cahill (1976) Limited, Dublin.

Cover design by Steven Hope

Nihil Obstat:
Richard Sherry D.D.,
Censor Deputatus.

Imprimatur:
✠ Dermot,
Archbhishop of Dublin,
October 1977.

The *nihil obstat* and *imprimatur* are a declaration that
a text is considered to be free of doctrinal or moral
error. They do not necessarily imply agreement with
opinions expressed by the author.

ISBN 0 905092 46 5
Cat. No. 3367

Contents

1 Advent — a new beginning

The liturgical year begins on the first Sunday of
Advent. For the Church and all its members this
day should also mark a new beginning in the
Christian pilgrimage. The coming of the Son of
God into our world heralded a new age. In the
Book of Revelation Christ is heard to say:
"Behold, I make all things new" (*RV 21: 5*). As
the Church commemorates that coming in the
liturgy of Advent and Christmas, all the faithful
are called to renewal.

During the four weeks of Advent the Church
prepares spiritually and liturgically to celebrate
the Birthday of the Lord. Such preparation is
necessary if we are to celebrate Christmas worthily
and be renewed and enriched by it. Otherwise
the feast will come and go, leaving us unchanged
and no nearer to God than before. We must be
earnest in our preparation and strive to become
better people than we are; for, as Pope Pius XII
observed in his encyclical on the liturgy, "God
cannot worthily be honoured unless the mind
and will are intent upon spiritual perfection".[1]

At the beginning of this season the call to
conversion is addressed to all of us. How appropriate is that passage from the letter of St Paul

to the Romans *(13: 11-24)* which provides the
second reading for year A:

> You know the time has come: you must wake
> up now: our salvation is even nearer than it
> was when we were converted. The night is
> almost over, it will be daylight soon — let us
> give up all the things we prefer to do under
> cover of the dark; let us arm ourselves and
> appear in the light. Let us live decently as
> people do in the daytime . . . Let your armour
> be the Lord Jesus Christ.

These words were decisive in the conversion of
St Augustine, as we know from his *Confessions*.
Their note of urgency should not be lost on us.
They can also change our lives.

Advent is not penitential in the way that Lent
is. Joyful hope, rather than penance, is the keynote
of this season. It does not follow that we may
ignore or play down the ascetic element. The call
to penance, conversion, and renewal is very much
present. Indeed it is always present in the Christian
life, but, since human nature of itself will always
choose the way of least resistance, we need from
time to time to renew our Christian commitment.
Advent, like Lent, is a "favourable time" to undergo
a change of heart and to make a new and determined
advance in our spiritual journey.

St John the Baptist is very prominent in Advent.
He is an ideal companion, at once austere and
joyful. His own life was penitential in the extreme,
but there was no note of sadness in it. As the
herald and forerunner of the Lord, he rejoiced to

hear the voice of the Bridegroom. He is the one
to stir us out of our complacency: "Repent, for
the kingdom of heaven is close at hand", was his
cry.

St Matthew, reporting these words and describing
the ministry of John, sees here fulfilled the prophetic utterance of Isaiah:

> A voice cries, "Prepare in the wilderness a way
> for the Lord. Make a straight highway for our
> God across the desert. Let every valley be filled
> in, every moutain and hill be laid low, let every
> cliff become a plain, and the ridges a valley . . ."
> (Is 40: 3-4).

Penance may be viewed as a task of spiritual
reclamation. If a piece of rough, uncultivated land
is to be made arable, it has to be reclaimed by
machinery and hard work. At the spiritual level,
something equally arduous and unremitting is
required. Only in this way can we prepare a way
for the Lord. This thought has inspired some of
the Advent prayers: "At your bidding, Lord, we
are preparing the way for Christ your Son. May
we not grow faint on our journey as we wait for
his healing presence"; and again: "Clear a pathway,
Lord, in our hearts to make ready for your only
Son, so that when he comes we may serve you in
sincerity of heart".[2]

Penance is not all our own work, it is primarily
the effect of God's grace in our souls. But if God
is to do his work in us, we must first remove the
obstacles which impede his action. If there are
barriers and "no-go areas" in our lives, these

must first be done away with. As free agents, using
our liberty responsibly, we must give God access to
our lives.

In Christ, the eternal Son, God has appeared
among us in human form. He seeks entry to our
inmost lives in order that he may share his life
with us. He stands at the gate and knocks, but
he does not force entry. The door to our hearts
can be opened only from the inside. St Charles
Borromeo says: "So now if we remove all barriers,
he is ready to come to us again at any minute or
hour to make his home spiritually within us with
all his grace".[3]

Christ may come at any time. His spiritual
advent is not confined to any particular
time or season. Indeed the mystery of Christ's
presence among us and within us, through the Holy
Spirit, is, in a very special sense, the grace of
Pentecost. And so it is that the fathers of the
Church loved to speak, in season and out of
season, of Christ's coming into the minds and
hearts of men. There is a beautiful reading in the
breviary in which we find the thoughts of St
Ambrose on this subject.[4] He, too, is very taken by
the image of Christ standing at the door of our
hearts, and says: "Let your door be open to him
when he comes, open your soul, throw open your
inmost minds, so that it may see the riches of
simplicity, the treasures of peace, the sweetness of
grace". And further on he exclaims: "Blessed,
therefore, is that man at whose door Christ knocks.
Our door is faith, which, if strong, fortifies the

whole house. It is through this door that Christ comes in".

It was St Bernard who connected this spiritual coming of Christ with Advent. In his sermons for this season he speaks of three comings of the Lord: his coming which has already taken place in the nativity, his future coming in glory, and his spiritual coming which belongs to the present. Of the latter he says: "This intermediary coming is like a road leading from the first to the last coming. In the first coming Christ was our redemption, in the last he will apear as our life; in this intermediary coming he is our rest and consolation".[5]

Christ will come again

Some are puzzled by the Advent liturgy, or by the explanations they have heard about it, for it would seem that we are trying to grapple with two or more ideas at once. Past, present, and future perspectives appear jumbled together. We have just dealt with the spiritual advent which appealed so much to St Bernard. Then there is the coming at a particular moment of time which we celebrate at Christmas: this presents no special difficulty. But there is another perspective, the future one, Christ's return in glory at the end of the ages, and it is here that we may find ourselves in difficulty. How are we to harmonise these various aspects?

It will be noted that on the first Sunday of Advent the gospel readings for the three years all refer to our Lord's second coming. We may wonder why this is so and what the connection is between Christ's coming nearly two thousand years ago and his return in the future at a time known only to the Father. On reflection, however, we discover that these two "comings" are inter-related and complementary. They may be viewed as two phases or aspects of the one saving mystery.

The fathers of the Church, faithful to scripture, did not dissociate these two comings, but considered them together and spoke of them almost in the same breath. An example of the patristic approach is given by St Cyril of Jerusalem who speaks to us of the twofold coming of Jesus Christ in the office of readings for the first Sunday. "We preach not one coming only of Christ", he says, " but a second also, far more glorious than the first". Then he goes on to contrast these two comings: "In the first coming he was wrapped in swaddling clothes in the manger. In his second coming he is clothed with light as with a garment. In the first coming he bore the cross, despising its shame; he will come a second time in glory accompanied by the hosts of angels".[6]

The very word "Advent" can be understood in two ways. It can mean a coming which has already taken place or one which is awaited: presence and expectation. In the New Testament the equivalent Greek work is *parousia,* which also can be translated as coming or arrival, but more often it refers to the second coming of Christ, the Day of the Lord.[7] If the meaning of our liturgical Advent is somewhat imprecise, this is all to the good since it helps us to consider together the two aspects of the one mystery. As Karl Rahner has observed: "The event which we call 'the second coming' is not so much a second arrival as a bringing to perfect completion of God's own life established in the world by the Christ event".[8]

There is no make-belief about Advent. We do not have to imagine that we are living in the ages before Christ. We cannot project ourselves into Old Testament times as though we still awaited a messiah and saviour. The long night of waiting is over and the fulness of time has come. The Word was made flesh and has dwelt among us. He is Emmanuel, "God is with us". And yet the Church continues to wait and to hope: "To you, my God, I lift up my soul", she sings on the first Sunday of Advent. She awaits and longs for the fulness of Christ's coming. The world has been redeemed but the history of redemption continues. It will continue until Christ the Lord has brought his task to completion. The kingdom of God has not yet been fully established and the work of extending the reign of Christ on earth must continue.

It is in this intermediate time, between Pasch and Parousia, that the Old Testament prophets can help us. Their hopes and aspirations we can appropriate for ourselves. Transformed in the full light of revelation, they become even more real for the people of God of the New Covenant than for the people of old. The messianic longing, so powerfully evoked by Isaiah, is perfectly suited to express the Church's most deep-felt hopes and aspirations.

2 Season of hope

Advent is the season of hope. The liturgy of this time is a continuous canticle of hope. Its spirit is summed up in an antiphon which is quite typical: "Lift up your eyes, Jerusalem, and see the power of the king. Behold, the Saviour comes. He will free you from your bonds".

"He will come again in glory to judge the living and the dead, and his kingdom will have no end". Such is the hope of the Church which we profess each Sunday at Mass. Let us say these words with conviction. Ours should be the attitude of the early Christians who lived in joyful expectation of the return of the Lord. This attitude is voiced in the exclamation which concludes the New Testament and which was the favourite prayer of the primitive Church: "Come, Lord Jesus".

In medieval times the final judgment was depicted in art and literature in a somewhat horrific manner. Such was the sombre spirit of the time. The Day of the Lord was *dies irae, dies illa*, "the day of wrath", as expressed in the sequence for funeral masses. It was a day to be feared and dreaded. In such a view Christ appears more in his role of Judge than of Saviour. There is an imbalance here. That there is to be a judgment is certain, and it is to be taken seriously. The outcome for each one of us will depend on our relationship with Christ at the hour of our death. Our Judge will also be our Saviour. The time and the manner of that judgment is not for us to ascertain. Its significance is summed up in the words of Romano Guardini: "In the end truth will conquer, and each and everything will be evalued according to its true worth".

Christians of today are more attracted by the spirituality of the early Church with its attitude of joyful optimism. The Church is more conscious than in the past that she is a pilgrim Church and that her hope lies in the future. She looks forward to the restoration of all things in Christ and to a new heaven and a new earth; only then will she attain her full perfection. This aspect of the Church's vocation has been strongly emphasised by the second Vatican Council.[1] It is the eschatological aspect which is given frequent expression in the new liturgy. After the words of institution in the Mass we have the acclamation, "Christ has died, Christ has risen, Christ will come again". And then in the memorial prayer (*anamnesis*) which follows, we not only commemorate the mysteries already accomplished but look forward to the return of the Lord Jesus, "ready to greet him when he comes again". And, finally, at the moment of communion we are reminded that the eucharist is a foretaste of the eschatological banquet in words which echo St John: "Happy are those who are invited to the wedding feast of the Lamb" (*Rv 19: 9*).

The spirit of advent, which is a spirit of hope,

should animate our lives. What is a basic Christian attitude is but intensified during these weeks of preparation for Christmas. In the words of the Council: "Enlivened and united in his Spirit, we journey toward the consummation of human history, one which fully accords with the counsel of God's love: 'To re-establish all things in Christ, both those in heaven and those on the earth' *(EP 1: 10)*".[2]

It is true that hope is a difficult virtue to practise in the time we live in. So much militates against it. Man's hope of a better world through science and technology has received a knocking in recent decades; confidence in progress and civilization has been undermined. The virtue of Christian hope has likewise been sorely put to the test. Religious institutions are under attack, moral values are in decline, materialism and secularism are in the ascendancy. What future then is there for Christianity, what hope is there for the Church?

Humanly speaking there is little enough cause for hope; but Christian hope is not based on merely human considerations but on God's goodness and power. In spite of human malice and failure, God's plan for the world is irreversible and is carried forward no matter how great the forces are that oppose it. That plan is centred on Christ who is the Lord of history. He is the power and the wisdom of God who carries out his designs *fortiter et suaviter,* "with strength and gentleness", as we declare in the first of the Great Antiphons. The

divine plan for the salvation of the human race
goes steadily forward.

It is this religious hope which makes the
Christian an optimist even in wordly matters.
It enables us to recognise and to value all that is
good and worthwhile in the achievements of
humankind. The search for a more just society, for
greater fellowship among nations, for a more
equitable distribution of the world's goods, all
these represent real gains and are harbingers of
hope. In the religious sphere one can only rejoice
in the positive signs of the Spirit's activity in the
Church. The renewal brought about by Vatican II
is one such sign. The drawing together of the
Churches in the ecumenical movement is another
powerful sign. Perhaps the most impressive sign
of all is the rediscovery of prayer in what is called
the charismatic movement. For all these we should
humbly give thanks to God.

The people of God must play their part in build-
ing a better world and in preparing a way for the
Lord. The two tasks go together. It is not the
Christian attitude to fold one's arms and to "wait
for better times". The pastoral Constitution on
the Church in the Modern World makes it quite
clear that we are committed both to the city of
God and to the city of men. It declares: "They are
mistaken who, knowing that we have here no
abiding city but seek one which is to come, think
that they may therefore shirk their earthly re-
sponsibilities".[3]

"Watch and pray"

In the market place of the old German town of
Trier, two church towers stand close together.
Beneath the belfry of each stands a Latin inscription. One reads. "Watch and pray" the other
completes the quotation, " For you know not the
day nor the hour". As they chime out the passing
hours we are reminded of the transitoriness of life
and of the need for vigilance.

Watching or vigilance is a very important but
rather neglected virtue. Its importance has been
stressed by our Lord himself and by his apostles.
In a sermon entitled "Watching", Cardinal
Newman draws attention to this and illustrates
his theme with quotations from the New Testament. Unlike other Christian virtues, such as
hoping and believing, "watching" is an attitude
of mind and heart which eludes precise definition.
Its meaning is not obvious, but its characteristics
in the one who practises it may thus be described:

He watches for Christ who has a sensitive,
eager, apprehensive mind; who is awake, alive,
quick-sighted, zealous in honouring him; who
looks out for him in all that happens, and
who would not be surprised, who would not
be over-agitated or overwhelmed, if he found
that he was coming at once . . . This then is to
watch; to be detached from what is present, and
to live in what is unseen; to live in the thought
of Christ as he came once, and as he will come
again; to desire his second coming, from our

affectionate and grateful remembrance of his
first.[4]

Watching, then, means living in the thought of
Christ's second coming. It should be an abiding
attitude of mind, governing all our behaviour.
A virtue for all seasons, but especially appropriate
during Advent.

The motto of the Catholic boy scouts of Ireland is "Bí ollamh" (Be ready), meaning readiness
to be of service to others; and their custom of
holding the right hand raised during the reading
of the gospel at Mass also indicates their willing-
ness to be of service to Christ. If we are ready at
all times to be of service to our neighbour and to
God, then we are practising vigilance; we are
watching for Christ.

This watching is not anxious but patient and
peaceable, while at the same time alert. It is the
watchfulness of the night nurse who, without
fuss, is attentive to every unaccustomed sound or
sudden call. Patience is one of the qualities of
watching. It is not for us "to know the times or
dates that the Father has decided by his own
authority" *(Acts 1:7)*. We do not know if the Lord's
return is imminent, but we should live as if it
were. St James suggests that we adopt the attitude
of the farmer waiting for his crops to ripen:
"Think of a farmer: how patiently he waits for the
precious fruit of the ground until it has had the
autumn rains and the spring rains! You too have to
be patient; do not lose heart because the Lord's
coming will be soon" *(Jm 5: 7)*. The Church, like

the good farmer, knows how to wait; so should we.

This waiting kindles desire, the desire to see and to possess God. At least three of the patristic readings for Advent treat of this desire for God. St Anselm, on Friday of the first week, gives passioned expression to this sentiment: "Teach me to seek you, and reveal yourself to me as I seek, because I can neither seek you if you do not teach me how, nor find you unless you reveal yourself. Let me seek you in desiring you; let me find you in loving you; let me love you in finding you".[5] This desire to see God is born of love, and love knows no obstacles. That is how St Peter Chrysologus considers it in a sermon read on Thursday of the second week: "The law of love has no thought about what will be, what ought to be or what can be . . . Love cannot bear not to have sight of what it loves . . . That is why love that longs to see God has the spirit of devotion even though it lacks judgment".[6] St Augustine who, in his own life, discovered that our hearts are restless until they rest in God, explains this desire as a continuous prayer and crying out to God: "This very desire of yours is your prayer. If your desire is continual your prayer is continual too . . . If you do not want to cease praying, do not cease longing. Your unceasing desire is your unceasing voice".[7]

There are many people today who hunger for God. The apparent absence of God (the "God is dead" mentality) has left a void in their lives, a void they try to fill up with whatever rewards the world has to offer. The young turn to exotic Eastern cults in a search for religious experience. The resort to drugs is the last desperate bid for even momentary happiness. Pope Paul had this problem in mind, and especially the problem of the young, in his address of welcome to the Archbishop of Canterbury on the occasion of Dr Coggan's visit in April 1977:[8]

> It is the experience of all of us that the world desperately needs Christ. The young, in whose aspirations good is often seen most vividly, feel this need most strongly. Secular optimism does not satisfy them. They are waiting for a proclamation of hope. Now is our chance to bear witness together that Christ is indeed the way, and the truth and the life, and that he is communicated through the Holy Spirit.

In their joint statement, Pope and Archbishop, pledging themselves to work for reconciliation and unity in the Lord, declared: "Christian hope manifests itself in prayer and action — in prudence but also in courage".

Those of us who are secure in the faith must also *wait* for God; that is a condition of our calling. In an essay entitled "Waiting", Paul Tillich has some thought-provoking things to say.[9] He shows how, in our relationship with God, there must always be an element of waiting; of giving and not having at the same time. He says: "We are stronger when we wait than when we possess. When we possess God (or think we do), we reduce him to that small thing we knew and grasped of him; and we make it an idol . . . But if we know that we do not know him, and if we wait for him to make himself known to us, we then really know something of him, we then are grasped and known and possessed by him".

Let us now return to the liturgy and see how this idea of waiting and watching and longing finds expression in the prayers. We wait "in faith and love" says one of the Advent prayers: "Grant to us who in faith and love wait for his coming your gift of grace and the reward of true freedom".[10] Another prayer describes that waiting as "alert and watchful";[11] another speaks of longing for Christ: "Support us now and always as we wait, longing with all our hearts, for the coming of Christ, your son".[12] In the second Advent preface we express the desire that when Christ comes "he may find us watching in prayer, our hearts filled with wonder and praise".

To this idea of waiting for Christ must be added the more expressive thought of going out to meet him when he comes. This idea, suggested by the parable of the ten bridesmaids (*Mt. 25: 1-13*), has inspired some of the prayers: "Grant, almighty Father, that when Christ comes again, we may go out to meet him, bearing the harvest of good works achieved by your grace".[13] Another expresses it thus: "Almighty and merciful God, let neither our daily work nor the cares of this life prevent us from hastening to meet your Son".[14] Even closer to the parable is the following: "Lord, keep us ever alert and watchful as we await the coming of your Son, so that, faithful to his teaching, we may hasten to meet our Saviour with lamps alight".[15]

3 Our Lady in Advent

Throughout the whole Advent season we feel the presence of the Virgin Mary. She remains discreetly in the background, but her influence is all-pervasive. Her role in the unfolding of God's plan is all-important, but is entirely subordinate to that of her divine Son. Liturgically speaking, December has a greater claim to be called "Mary's month" than the month of May, although it is fitting too that popular devotion dedicates the most beautiful time of the year to the Mother of the Lord.

It is the scene of the Annunciation which is most constantly in the Church's thought during Advent. This scene is commemorated, sometimes evoked in a dramatic way, in the liturgy. Its importance in the plan of salvation is thus highlighted. According to Catholic tradition, Mary's *fiat*, her unqualified "yes" to the role God had chosen for her, was of decisive importance in the bringing to fruition of God's plan for the salvation of mankind. In the words of the Second Vatican Council: "The Virgin Mary, when the angel brought the news, welcomed the Word of God in her heart and in her body and brought life into the world"; and, further on in its Constitution on the Church, it adds: "Embracing God's saving will with a full heart and impeded by no sin, she devoted herself totally as a handmaid of the Lord to the person and work of her Son. In subordination to him along with him, by the grace of almighty God she has served the mystery of redemption".[1]

In the liturgy we re-live the scene of the Annunciation, we overhear the dialogue between the angel and virgin and we experience the suspense of that moment before the word of consent is spoken: "Virgin Mary, receive the word of the Lord brought to you by the angel: You will conceive and bear a son, both God and man. You will be called Blessed among all women. . ." (Responsory for Office of Readings, 20 December).

St Bernard, in his characteristic way, expands imaginatively on the gospel narrative. Like other of the fathers before him, he believed that the Incarnation, and so the salvation of the world, depended on Mary's answer. And so he addresses her as though he and we were present at that scene, and on our behalf he pleads with Mary that she may not withold her consent: "The angel is waiting for your answer: it is time for him to return to God who sent him. We too are waiting, O Lady, for the word of pity, even we who are overwhelmed in wretchedness by the sentence of damnation".[2]

It was a moment of decision, what we sometimes call the "moment of truth". There are such moments in our own lives, as when a young woman consents to marry the man who proposes to her; or when one renounces marriage and responds to a vocation to the religious life; or even the more ordinary decision of choosing a career. An option is taken and from that moment life takes on a new course. We set in motion a series of events which affect not only our own destiny but that of others as well.

The Virgin Mary did not hesitate, she only sought clarification: "How can this be?" There was no time to think things through, no possibility of foreseeing all the consequences of her decision. The prospect must indeed have been awesome. She did what only could be done in such circumstances: she made an act of faith and said Yes to God's proposal. The life she had lived until then must have been a preparation for that moment: such an act of faith and trust pre-supposes similar acts throughout her young life; and, as we know, her *fiat* would entail further innumerable acts of obedience which, though unforeseen, were included implicitly in the initial act of giving.

Her response was not only prompt and unreserved, but joyful as well. She responded joyfully to the Good News brought to her by the angel. She did so not just as an individual member of her race, but as representing Israel. In the thought of St Luke she personifies her people and so the Church. Moreover, since the divine plan embraced all peoples, she also represented the human race. On behalf of us all she accepted the divine gift and, in her, mankind assented to its salvation.

The fathers of the Church, beginning with St Irenaeus, marvelled at the obedience of Mary, and they have held up her act of obedience as a perfect example for all Christians. For Irenaeus, the Virgin's obedience remedied the disobedience of Eve and so she became the new Eve and the advocate of the one who had been deceived by the serpent.[3] St Augustine declared that the Virgin Mary conceived the Son of God in her mind and heart before she conceived him in her body *(prius concepit mente quam corpore).*[4] Her divine motherhood is, in the thought of St Augustine, the fruit of her obedient faith.

Mary is present throughout Advent, and this will become even more apparent in the final period when we meet her in the mystery of the Presentation. She possesses the secret of this season. Her waiting was also a bringing forth, it was the personal Advent of a mother waiting for her child to be born. In the words of the preface, "she bore him in her womb with love beyond all telling". In her the hope of Israel was realised.

Advent is the season of hope, and we invoke Our Lady as *Mater spei,* "Mother of hope". She is the hope of the Church and of each individual member of it. In her present state of glory, perfectly united in body and soul with the Lord, we see to what heights we too are called. In the words of the Council: "In her the Church admires and holds aloft the most excellent fruit of redemption, and joyfully contemplates, as in a faultless image, that which she herself desires and hopes to be",[5] and "until the day of the Lord comes, she is certainly the resplendant sign of sure hope and comfort for the People of God on their pilgrimage".[6]

The feast of the Immaculate Conception is

placed like a jewel in the heart of the Advent season. Historically speaking, that is by accident rather than by design since the date is determined by the more ancient feast of the Nativity of the Virgin (8 September); it falls just nine months before the latter. From the liturgical point of view, however, it is very appropriate that it should be celebrated at this time.

This feast celebrates the perfect holiness of the Blessed Virgin Mary. It affirms the Church's belief that Mary, from the very moment of her conception, was preserved free from all stain of original sin. It was fitting that the mother of the Incarnate Word should thus be prepared for her role in the work of redemption. She was to be the new Ark of the Covenant and Tabernacle of God. This unique privilege of Mary — her Immaculate Conception — we attribute to the foreseen merits of her Son. She too was redeemed by Christ her Son, the universal Saviour. In the words of the prayer, Mary was preserved from the stain of sin and prepared to be the Mother of God "by the power of Christ's redeeming death".

The feast, in its present form, was instituted by Pope Pius IX when he defined the dogma of the Immaculate Conception on 8 December 1854.

4 Rejoice in the Lord

As Advent enters its final phase, the Church's joy knows no bounds. This note of joy, present if subdued from the beginning of the season, first breaks out on the third Sunday of Advent. We have reached the mid-point of this time of preparation and the Church encourages us all to persevere. It was known as "Gaudete Sunday" from the opening word of the entrance song: *"Gaudete in Domino . . ."* ("Rejoice in the Lord"). If the name has not been retained, the joyful character of the liturgy is still much in evidence. We find it in the introit, the opening prayer, the readings and in the communion antiphon. Nowhere is the theme better illustrated than in the reading from St Paul's letter to the Philippians:

> I want you to be happy, always happy in the Lord; I repeat, what I want is your happiness. Let your tolerance be evident to everyone: the Lord is very near. There is no need to worry; but if there is anything you need, pray for it, asking God for it with prayer and thanksgiving, and that peace of God, which is so much greater than we can understand, will guard your hearts and your thoughts, in Christ Jesus (*Ph 4: 4-7*).[1]

St Paul was a realist, and these lines were written when he was a prisoner. He cannot be accused of wishful thinking or old man's euphoria; but in his captivity he came to experience more profoundly the nearness of the Lord and this was for him an immense source of hope and joy. This discovery becomes a message of hope for the church at Philippi; it is a message which continues to strengthen and console. In our own experience of the presence of Christ in our lives, cares and problems do not vanish but they appear of much less account.

Aemeliana Löhr, commenting on the words "The Lord is very near" has the following reflection: "The Messias, saviour God, awaited by Jews and pagans alike, has come. God has redeemed his people, and not withdrawn from them again. He is here, in his Church; his living breath, his divine life are present in every one of the baptised; all who believe have his strength and love from which to live; everyone of us who takes part in his holy sacrifice grows in this fire-like undying life". And further on she says: "Living thus in the inward presence of the Lord, the Church knows, as does the individual, that Advent is at the same time the Lord's presence and his coming. She breathes in his nearness and lives his life; thus she grows in sharing his inwardness. Because she has him she wishes to have him forever".[2]

The Book of Consolation

Throughout the four weeks of Advent, the Prophet

Isaiah is read. Rightly so, since he is the greatest of the messianic prophets. The sign of the virgin who will conceive and bear a son whose name is Emmanuel, is one of the better known of his prophecies (*Is 7: 10-17*); but there are others, equally important, which we have met in the readings of the lectionary and breviary.[3] But between these and other consoling texts there is much warning and reproach, oracles against the nations, diatribes against his own people and its rulers. Isaiah can be stern and even menacing, even if his underlying message is one of absolute trust in God.

Now, towards the end of Advent the readings of the office are taken from that portion of Isaiah which is known as "the Book of the consolation of Israel". This comprises chapters 40-55, and, according to scholars, it is the work of a later disciple of the prophet. The Jewish people are in exile. What they need now is not warnings but a message of hope. This prophetic work was just what was needed to give comfort and hope to a dispirited people. It proclaims a great deliverance from the present captivity, a new exodus of the people of God as wonderful as the first. They would return in triumph to their land and God would rebuild Jerusalem.

The tone of the work is set from the beginning in those words of comfort which we find strangely moving:

Comfort, comfort my people says your God.
Speak tenderly to Jerusalem, and cry to her

that her warfare is ended, that her iniquity
is pardoned, that she has received from the
Lord's hand double for all her sins.
(*Is 40: 1-2, RSV version*).

It is on this note of sustained hope and joy
that the Church concludes her preparation for
Christmas.

Immediate Preparation

The time of immediate preparation for Christmas
can be dated from 17 December. From this date
the liturgy acquires a distinctive form and is
designed to lead us progressively day by day to the
feast of Christmas.

It may be of interest to know why this particular
day was chosen to begin the Church's final preparation. There is an historical reason. It seems
that at an early period in the Western Church,
before the Roman Advent was organised in the
sixth century, the churches of Christian Gaul and
Spain began their preparation for Christmas and
Epiphany on 17 December. This was just three weeks
before the Epiphany, a feast of very great importance in Gaul, as it was in the East, and a day
on which baptism was conferred. So we have here
the vestige of a more ancient Advent which began
on this day and concluded three weeks later on
the Epiphany.[4]

Historical considerations aside, we have eight
days of intensive preparation for Christmas. It
may help us to think of this period as correspond-

ing in some way to Holy Week. It remains for us
now to examine the various elements in the liturgy
of this time.

The daily office begins with the invitatory
antiphon: "The Lord is at hand: come, let us adore
him". This refrain is re-echoed in the Benedictus
antiphon: "Know that the kingdom of God is at
hand; be sure that he will not delay". On the
following morning it is the same cry: "Watch, the
Lord is near".

As Christmas approaches the Church seems to
count the days, as we ourselves counted the days
to the holidays when we were at school. Take the
antiphon for morning prayer on the 21st. There are
just five days to the feast, and the Church exclaims: "Do not be afraid. You will see our Lord
on the fifth day". On the 23rd everything is in
readiness, as it was for the first Christmas, and we
can sing in the Benedictus antiphon: "Behold
everything is fulfilled which the angel promised
the Virgin Mary".

We arrive at Christmas eve. The liturgy appro-
priates passages from the Old Testament to express
the imminence of Christ's coming. In the invitatory
antiphon we exclaim: "Know today that the Lord
will come; in the morning you will see his glory".
This is actually taken from the Book of Exodus
and, in its original context, refers to the miraculous
feeding of the Israelites in the desert. The Lord,
promising the manna to Moses, given him instruction
for the people: "So Moses and Aaron said to all
the people of Israel, 'At evening you shall know
that it was the Lord who brought you out of the

land of Egypt, and in the morning you shall see
the glory of the Lord" *(Ex 16: 6)*.

These texts place us in the context of salvation
history. The imagery of the passover and exodus
throw light on the mystery we are about to celebrate. The events of the New Covenant are in
continuity with the old. Salvation history is a
continuing process, and it is as a mystery of salvation
that the liturgy presents the feast of Christmas:
"Lift up your heads for your redemption is at
hand"; "Tomorrow your salvation will be with
you, says the Lord God Almighty" (antiphons
from morning prayer). It is especially in the short
responsory that the Nativity appears in a paschal
and redemptive light: "Tomorrow is the day on
which the sins of the world will be wiped away.
The Saviour of the world will rule us himself".[5]

The Great Antiphons

In the office of evening prayer, the *Magnificat* canticle is adorned with those wonderful compositions
popularly known as the "O antiphons". They are
so called because in each of the seven antiphons
Christ, the Incarnate Word, is addressed by a
divine or messianic title, "O Wisdom", "O Adonai",
"O stock of Jessa", etc. Each is a prayer to this
Word of God who has existed with the Father and
Holy Spirit from all eternity and has now become
man and dwelt among us. The Church recalls his
saving role in the history of his people, his presence
and activity as the second Divine Person, even in
the Old Testament, and, having commemorated

his mercies in the past, the Church prays that
he may come anew to heal, enlighten, and save our
world.

The Great Antiphons have been in use in the
Roman Church from the eighth century. The
author, whose identity is unknown, must have
been deeply versed in the sacred scriptures, for in
these compositions he has skillfully woven together
passages of the Old Testament and, in doing so, has
created something new. (In giving the text of these
antiphons below, we have included the biblical
references.)

In monasteries it has long been the custom to
sing these antiphons, with their majestic melodies,
to the accompaniment of the organ and the ringing
of the church bells. The priest, who intones the
antiphon, wears alb and cope an incenses the altar
during the singing of the magnificat; and so the
O antiphons are significant not only for their text
and music but also for the imposing ceremonial
which surrounds them.

Cardinal Newman had evidently a great love for
these antiphons. In his daily visits to the Blessed
Sacrament it was his custom to say a prayer of
his own composition to Christ present in the
eucharistic mystery. Having said this prayer, expressing his own deep faith in the real presence, he
would then recite one of the O antiphons, a
different one for each day beginning with the "O
Sapientia" on Sunday.[6]

Fr Pierre Jounel, the well-known French liturgist
writes: "The Great Antiphons are not only a syn-
thesis of the purest messianic hope of the Old

Testament: by means of the ancient images of the Bible, they enumerate the divine titles of the Incarnate Word, and their *Veni* ("come") expresses all the present longing of the Church. In them the liturgy of Advent reaches its summit".[7]

Here now are the antiphons as translated in the *Divine Office*. It may be noted that they have also found their way into the liturgy of the word at Mass; they may be used from 17 December to Christmas eve as Alleluia verses, and in this way they are brought to the attention of larger numbers of the faithful.

17 December (*O Sapientia*). O Wisdom, you came forth from the mouth of the Most High (*Ecc. 24: 3*). You fill the universe and hold all things together in a strong yet gentle manner (*Wisdom 8: 1*). O come to teach us the way of truth (*Isaiah 40: 14*).

18 December (*O Adonai*). O Adonai and leader of Israel (*Matthew 2: 6*), you appeared to Moses in a burning bush and you gave him the Law on Sinai. O come and save us with your mighty power (*Jeremiah 32: 21*).

19 December (*O Radix Jesse*). O stock of Jesse, you stand as a signal for the nations *(Isaiah 11:10)*; Kings fall silent before you whom the peoples acclaim (*Is 52: 15*). O come to deliver us, and do not delay (*Habacuc 2: 3*).

20 December (*O Clavis David*). O key of David and sceptre of Israel, what you open no one else can close again; what you close no one can open (*Isaiah 22: 22*). O come to lead the captive from

prison; free those who sit in darkness and in the shadow of death (*Psalm 106: 10*).

21 December (*O Oriens*). O Rising Sun, you are the splendour of eternal light (*Habacuc 3: 4*) and the sun of justice (*Malachy 4: 2*). O come and enlighten those who sit in darkness and in the shadow of death (*Luke 1: 78*).

22 December (*O Rex Gentium*). O King whom all the peoples desire (*Haggai 2: 8*), you are the cornerstone which makes all one (*Ephesians 2: 20*). O come and save man whom you made from clay (*Genesis 2: 7*)

23 December (*O Emmanuel*). O Emmanuel, you are our king and judge, (*Isaiah 33: 22*), the one whom the peoples await and their Saviour (*Genesis 49: 10*). O come and save us, Lord, our God.

That final plea, "O come and save us, Lord, our God, sums up all the preceding petitions. It is a cry from the heart of the Church and, since the Church prays not only for herself but for the world, it is also a cry from the heart of mankind. How universal and all-embracing is this ancient prayer!

In spite of their antiquity there is something timeless about the O antiphons. Because they express so well our own deep spiritual hunger and all the problems and anxieties that beset us, they are as relevant today as in the past. It is a truism that human nature does not change; it is equally true that human needs remain basically the same.

We live in a world where there is much suffering

and want, where sin abounds and all the miseries
that are a consequence of sin. There are those who
"sit in darkness and the shadow of death", the
darkness of ignorance, disbelief, and blind pre-
judice. There are the "captives in prison", those
enslaved by their own passions, greed, and
ambition; those who enslave others to further
their own selfish ends.

When we look into our own lives we realise that all
is not right; our own house needs to be put in
order. To the extent that sin has a hold over us we,
too, are enslaved and in darkness. We, too, need to
be set free from all that holds us in bondage. We,
too, need the light and the healing power of Christ.
We turn then in prayer to Christ, Son of God and
son of Mary, to him who holds the key to our own
lives and destinies. May he shed his light on our
minds and understanding, dispel from our hearts
the darkness of sin, bring us out of our prison
house and make us truly free with the freedom of
God's children.

These prayers are not only timeless but also
universal in scope. They express the universal need
of salvation. Man is not self-sufficient. He is in
need of a saviour, and, whether he recognises him
or not, that Saviour is Christ. He is "the one whom
the peoples await and their Saviour". We pray that
he may come into the lives of those who have not
yet believed in him, and we pray too for those many
millions among whom Christ cannot be preached.

The prospect of an earthy paradise without God is
illusory, and modern man has begun to shed his
illusions. While there is real progress on many fronts,

it does not go deep enough. Basic human problems remain unsolved. Nations have not found an alternative to war in resolving their conflicts. Peace, no matter how great the efforts to secure it, keeps eluding us. Civilization comes not in a steady flow but like the ebb and flow of the waves on the sea shore. The welfare state has not rid our cities and towns of violence.

The Church, strong in faith, and serene in hope, calls on Christ, the Saviour of all men, to deliver us from all that oppresses us and to teach us the way of truth.

Readings at Mass

During the last week of Advent, the readings at Mass all have a direct bearing on the mystery of the nativity. They illustrate it by describing other wonderful births, such as that of the prophet Samson and that of John the Baptist. They also recount the events leading up to it: Mary's betrothal to Joseph, the angel's message, and the visit to Elizabeth.

Each day the liturgy of the word has a unified theme. The Old Testament reading harmonises with the gospel. Another interesting feature is that when we open our breviaries we find the gospel theme carried over into the Office of Readings; the message of the Mass is thus meditated upon in the liturgy of the hours. Let us now look at these readings.

17 December. The gospel (*Mt 1: 1-17*) proclaims

the genealogy of Jesus Christ, son of David. This serves as a solemn opening to this week of preparation.

18 December. The first reading (*Jer 23: 5-8*) foretells a "virtuous branch of David" who will reign as a wise and just king. The gospel (*Mt 1: 18-24*) describes the betrothal of Mary and Joseph, the message of the angel, fulfilment of the prophecy: Mary will conceive and give birth to a Son; he is to be called Jesus for he will "save his people from their sins"; he is also Emmanuel, a name which means "God-is-with-us".

19 December. If the birth of Jesus is unique and without precedent, it is nonetheless prefigured by two other wonderful births, both of which are commemorated in today's readings. The birth of Samson was also announced by an angel, to the mother who was barren the good news was brought: "You will conceive and bear a son". The gospel (*Lk 1: 5-25*) describes an even more wonderful birth, that of John the Baptist. His parents were old, his mother Elizabeth barren. The angel Gabriel announces the good news to Zechariah. His wife will bear a son who is to be called John, and even from his mother's womb he will be filled with the Holy Spirit.

20 December. Again we find a correspondence between the two readings. It is the connection of prophecy and fulfilment. In the first, Isaiah (*7: 10-14*) foretells that "the maiden is with child and will soon give birth to a son whom she will

call Immanuel". In the gospel (*Lk 1: 26-38*), re-
cording the annunciation, we see that prophecy
fulfilled. Notice in the Divine Office St Bernard's
beautiful homily on the mystery of the annunciation, and also the prayer of the day which is inspired by this same theme.

21 December. Here the scene moves from the
annunciation to the visitation (*Lk 1: 39-45*). Here
Mary is seen as the one who is always prompt
to carry out God's will, hurrying to render
humble service to her elderly cousin. We idealise
the scene but the journey to the hill country must
have been exhausting. Then the meeting of the two
cousins, a scene so familiar to us as to require no
description but the significance of which is so profound. In that mysterious meeting, so rich in
prophetic utterance, in outpouring of grace, in
joyful thanksgiving in the Holy Spirit, there is
much to meditate on. St Ambrose, in the Office
of Readings, seeks to unlock for us the mystery.
What is interesting in his commentary is the way
he associates us with Mary in her life and vocation
and in the mysteries she shares with her Son.
Commenting on Elizabeth's greeting to Mary,
he addresses all of us in these words: "But you too,
who have heard and have believed are blessed.
Every soul who has believed both conceives and
generates the Word of God and recognises his
works".[8]

22 December. The readings today may be described as a liturgy of thanksgiving. First it is

Hannah giving thanks for Samuel's birth (*Sam 1: 24-28*); she brings him to the temple and, in gratitude to God who has heard her prayer, she makes the child over to the Lord for the rest of his life. The responsorial text which follows this reading gives us Hannah's song of thanksgiving, "My heart exults in the Lord, I find my strength in my God". This prepares us for the gospel (*Lk 1: 46-56*) which gives in full Mary's canticle of thanksgiving, the *Magnificat*. In the liturgy this canticle has become the Church's thanksgiving for the gift of redemption. St Ambrose would have us sing it in association with Mary: "Let the soul of Mary be in each one to magnify the Lord. Let the spirit of Mary be in each one to exult in God".

23 December. The readings are about John the Baptist. The prophet Malachi foretells the return of Elijah and describes his mission. Our Lord would later say that Elijah had come again in the person of John the Baptist: "he, if you will believe me, is the Elijah who was to return (*Mt 11: 14*). His role as forerunner is announced; he is the messenger who will prepare a way for the Lord. Then in the gospel St Luke narrates all the wonderful happenings which surround the birth of John. The people's sense of awe at this mysterious birth is voiced in that final question: "What will this child turn out to be?"

Finally on Christmas eve, Zechariah in the gospel (*Lk 1: 67-69*) sings his canticle of thanksgiving for the birth of John. In doing so he foretells John's prophetic role: "to go before the Lord to prepare the way for him; to give his people knowledge of salvation through forgiveness of their sins". On this note of thanksgiving the time of preparation is ended. The Advent liturgy has led us to the threshold of Christmas and it is this mystery we must now consider.

5 Christmas through the ages

A brief account of the origin and development of Christmas may help our understanding of the feast as we celebrate it in our time. In the religious, as in the secular sphere, the present cannot be fully understood without the light of the past.[1]

There is no mention of a feast of Christmas before the fourth century. In a Roman calendar, compiled by a certain Philocalus in 354 AD, we find the first clear reference. At the head of the list of feasts then celebrated there stands the simple inscription: "On 25 December, Christ is born in Bethlehem of Judaea". On the basis of this evidence, the institution of this feast is traced back to the early years of the fourth century.

The New Testament does not indicate the time of the year when Christ was born, although St Luke is careful to situate that event at a precise moment of history. He tells us, for example, that it occurred while Quirinius was governor of Syria (*Lk 2: 12*), and that was roughly between the years 8 and 6 BC. So in point of historical fact Jesus was not born *anno domino* 1 but earlier.[2]

The choice of this particular day was determined by a pre-Christian festival in Rome, that of the "Invincible Sun". According to the calculations of the time, 25 December was the date of the winter solstice. It was the day when the sun appeared at its weakest. This great source of light and heat seemed to be vanquished and at the point of death; but at that very moment it revived and day by day, almost imperceptibly, grew stronger and brighter. It proved itself to be unconquered and unconquerable. It was the emperor Aurelian who introduced to Rome the pagan festival of the *Sol Invictus* ("unconquered" or "invincible sun"). That was in the year 274 AD.

Such is the pre-Christian origin of Christmas. At first we are rather taken aback to learn that this most Christian of feasts should have pagan associations. On reflection, however, we discover here just one more instance of the Church's missionary and catechetical method. Rather than suppress existing customs and institutions, the Church prefers, whenever possible, to retain them but to invest them with new meaning. The Church of fourth-century Rome did not suppress the *Natalis solis invicti* ("Birthday of the unconquered sun") but transformed it into the *natalis Christi* ("Birthday of Christ"). The date is the same and the symbolism of light is still much in evidence, but the content is entirely new.

The symbolism of light and the sun was already familiar to Christians, a symbolism rooted in the Bible. Christ was already known as "Sun of Justice", "Splendour of the Father", "Light of the world", "Dawn from on high". A fourth-century writer, alluding to the now supplanted feast of the Invincible Sun, asks rhetorically: "But who is

invincible like our Lord who overcame and con-
quered death?" This writer included in his understanding of the feast not only the nativity of our
Lord but also his struggle with, and victory over,
Satan. On the cross Jesus seemed to lose the battle,
just as the winter sun seemed to be vanquished by
the darkness; but then, in his resurrection, he
conquers death and the powers of darkness and,
like the morning sun, rises to new life.

From this examination of origins, two important
ideas should be retained. Firstly, that Christmas is
a feast of light, a light which is not an object of
worship but a symbol of Christ who is the Light
of the world. Secondly, that this feast, since it
celebrates the victory of light over darkness, has
a redemptive character and so bears a relationship
to Easter, the feast of redemption.

The institution of this feast in fourth-century
Rome was effective in weaning the converts to
Christianity from any lingering attachment to
their pagan gods. Within the Church itself, it
helped to bolster the orthodox Christian faith
in the face of heresy. In 325 AD the Council of
Nicea condemned the Arian heresy which denied
the Divinity of Jesus. This council affirmed that
Jesus was "of one substance with the Father".
The celebration of Christmas, with its clear teaching on the divinity of Christ, was a powerful
affirmation of the Church's faith.

When the feast of Christmas was first introduced
to Rome, it was celebrated in a rather simple way.
It had no period of preparation and no octave.
Moreover, it had only a single Mass which took

place in the morning. How then did the three
Masses come about? The first thing to note is that
the so-called "day Mass", the one that is listed
third in the missal, is in fact the oldest and most
important of the celebrations. The gospel taken
from the prologue of St John's gospel, sets before
us the essential object of the feast, which is the
mystery of the Incarnation.

The Mass at midnight originated in this way.
The idea of a midnight celebration was borrowed
from Jerusalem. The pilgrim Egeria, in her *journal*,
describes such a service held at the grotto in Bethlehem. This took place, not on Christmas Day, but
on the feast of the Epiphany. The people assembled
there for midnight Mass, and then, early in the
morning, they returned to Jerusalem where a
second Mass was said.

Sometime in the fifth century a similar custom
was introduced to Rome. On the night before
Christmas the pope would celebrate Mass in a
chapel of the basilica of St Mary Major's. This
chapel bore the name, *ad Praesepe* ("at the crib
chapel"). It commemorated the grotto of Bethlehem. One can observe here the tendency in
Christian piety to commemorate the time and
the place of Christ's mysteries. The liturgy, now
as then, evokes the atmosphere of that first Christmas night. It is St Luke's account which is read
in the gospel (*2: 1-14*). This describes the humble
birth of Jesus "in a manger", the scene of the
shepherds watching their sheep by night, and the
appearance of the angels bringing them "news of
great joy".

The "Mass at dawn" was introduced in the sixth century. It was certainly known to Pope St Gregory the Great, who died in 604. In one of his homilies he refers to the three Masses he must celebrate at Christmas. Originally this second Mass was said in honour of a martyr, much honoured in the East, St Anastasia. Her feast was celebrated in Rome on this day in the basilica close by the imperial palace. Out of deference to the emperor, the pope felt obliged to celebrate a special Mass in honour of the martyr for the benefit of the court. In time this became simply a second Christmas Mass with just a commemoration of St Anastasia. In the recent reforms even this commemoration has been dropped.

Such is the origin of the three Masses which every priest has the privilege of saying on Christmas Day. What was at first the prerogative of the supreme pontiff was later extended to all the clergy. Each of these Masses has its distinctive character and provides a particular approach to the mystery. The scriptural and ecclesiastical texts provide a rich source of meditation. And, apart from the instruction they provide, the three Masses add splendour to this great feast and are a fitting homage to the Saviour who is born to us this day.

Once established, the feast of Christmas grew rapidly in rank and importance. From being a simple one-day commemoration, it developed into a liturgical cycle or season. Already by the second half of the fourth century it was joined by another nativity feast of eastern origin, the Epiphany. Two centuries later, the period of preparation, known as Advent, is firmly established in Rome. There too, about this time, the octave day of Christmas is celebrated: it commemorates the divine maternity of Mary. The feast of Epiphany also acquires an after-celebration so that by the seventh century the whole period of Advent, Christmas and Epiphany has acquired the form and content with which we are familiar today.

But if the liturgical history of Christmas is more-or-less complete by the beginning of the seventh century, there continues to be development in the realm of folk-custom and popular devotion. To give an account of the latter would require a chapter or even a book in itself; so let us record just a few of the customs and practices which, in the course of the centuries, have grown round the feast of the nativity.

The first custom which deserves mention is that of setting up a life-like crib in churches and homes. It seems that we owe this very attractive custom to St Francis of Assisi who in the year 1223 had the happy inspiration of arranging a very true-to-life *presepio* or crib for the benefit of the people of Greccio on Christmas Day. This was very much in accord with his own spirituality, so drawn to the poverty of Christ and to all that related to his humanity.

The singing of carols is also very much part of popular Christmas tradition. Here, too, we can discern the spirit of St Francis. He and the friars after him did much to propogate this form of popular hymnody. But carol-singing, as we know it today, is very much a product of the early nineteenth century revival, The most popular of these, "Stille Nacht" ("Holy Night") was sung for the first time in the parish church of Oberndorf in Austria at midnight Mass, Christmas 1818.

The exchange of gifts also belongs to the popular ritual of Christmas. This practice, together with the sending of Christmas cards, has in recent times got rather out of hand. The idea itself is good and in harmony with the spirit of Christmas. The original motivation was a religious one. It was, and still is in some countries, the custom to bring gifts to children on the feast of St Nicholas, 6 December, the saint who had provided dowries for a poor man's three daughters. In Germany, at the time of the Reformation, this custom was transferred to Christmas and the bringer of the gifts was no longer named as St Nicholas but as the *Christkind,* the "Christ Child".

Each country has its own customs associated with Christmas. It was the custom in Ireland to place a lighted candle by a window on Christmas night, as a sign of welcome to the holy family; also to leave the front door unlocked.

Leaving history aside, let us now direct our attention to the feast itself and, in the light of the liturgy, examine the profound truths it contains and then see how best we can apply this doctrine to our everyday Christian living.

6 The meaning of Christmas

The Word was made flesh

At the heart of our Christmas celebration lies the
mystery of the Incarnation. This constitutes the
essential object of the feast. St John, in the prologue to his gospel, declares this in one strong
affirmation: "The Word was made flesh, he lived
among us . . ." (*1: 14*). It is not just the birth of
Jesus at Bethlehem which is commemorated, nor
the circumstances of that birth, nor the events
surrounding it. It is, rather, the underlying mystery,
the mystery of God-made-man, which claims our
attention and engages our faith in the liturgy of
Christmas. This is, according to Newman, the
central truth of the gospel. It means that "the
eternal Son of God became by a second birth the
Son of God in time".[1]

As we meditate on this mystery, perhaps kneeling
before the crib, let us remember that the Child
on whom we gaze is not just a human child, nor is
he simply a divine Being in human guise. Rather
is he one who is both divine and human, the God-
man Jesus Christ. In the one Person of the Word,
a divine and a human nature are joined in a union
closer than anything we can conceive in the natural

order. This we call the hypostatic union. It means simply that Jesus Christ is true God and true man.

It is a mystery which exceeds human understanding and which makes great demands on our faith. Even where faith is strong and reason unquestioning, there is always the danger of misunderstanding the doctrine. It is not easy to maintain simultaneously and without imbalance the two truths, that Christ our Lord is true God and true man. Given the limitations of our understanding, it is not surprising that, consciously or unsconsciously, we over-emphasise one of these truths to the detriment of the other: either we think of Jesus only as God or we consider him solely in his humanity. The Church has always maintained the two sides of the mystery, and it is this whole and unified view that we find in the liturgy of Christmas.

Not that the Christmas liturgy is a systematic treatise on the doctrine of the Incarnation. That is not its function. It is, however, deeply theological. The Church teaches us, first of all, through the scriptures. In the readings for the three Christmas Masses and in other readings from the breviary, we find set before us some of the most important Christological texts of the New Testament. These are given for our instruction, to be read, to be thought about, and to be prayed over.

Next in importance to the scripture texts are the readings from the Church fathers. Among the latter we find St Athanasius (died 373), that great Spokesman of the Council of Nicea which declared Jesus to be of one substance with the Father; and also Pope St Leo (died 461), whose teaching on the doctrine of the Incarnation was acclaimed at the Council of Chalcedon in 451. These and other patristic texts, from Hippolytus to Bernard of Clairvaux, express the Church's understanding of the mystery.

In the hymns, antiphons, responsories and other such texts, the Church expresses in a more poetic form what is taught in the scriptures, the patristic readings and the creeds. But even these compositions are inspired by the psalms, the gospels and other parts of scripture and bear the stamp of the Church's dogmas. Take, for example, the following versicle and response: "The Word was made flesh, alleluia; and he lived among us, alleluia"; or this antiphon from evening prayer: "The Word was God in the beginning and before all time; today he is born to us, the Saviour of the world". In a rather more doctrinal form, the Benedictus antiphon for the octave day of Christmas expresses the mystery in words reminiscent of the Council of Chalcedon:[2]

Today a wonderful mystery is announced; something new has taken place; God has become man; he remained what he was and has become that which he was not; and though the two natures are distinct he is one.

It is indeed a wonderful mystery, something entirely new. In these days of Christmas we shall consider different aspects of that mystery. The first thing to marvel at is the divine condescension which the incarnation implies. In the antiphon for evening prayer 1, the Church exclaims: "The Word of God, born of the Father before time began, humbled himself today for us and became man". This antiphon introduces the great Christological hymn which speaks of the *kenosis* or self-emptying of Christ. It is from St Paul's letter to the Philippians (*2: 6-11*). We quote the first lines:

> Though he was in the form of God,
> Jesus did not count equality with God a thing to
>   be grasped.
> *He emptied himself,*
> taking the form of a servant,
> being born in the likeness of men.

We could dwell for a moment on that last line, "born in the likeness of men". (This is the RSV version. The Jerusalem Bible puts it more forcefully, "became as men are".) We may not realise the full implications of that statement, and, partly from a sense of reverence, we fail to do full justice to the humanity of Jesus. We must not fear to hold that Christ was truly a man, like us in all things, sin excluded. He had, in Newman's words, "a man's heart, a man's tears, and a man's wants and infirmities".[3] He became a man among men. He shared our human lot in every way. He experienced our joys and sorrows, our fears and anxieties.

To say that Christ became poor for our sake is another way of expressing the same mysterious reality. During the octave of Christmas we find this theme in a short passage from St Paul: "You know how generous our Lord Jesus Christ has been: he was rich, yet for your sake he became poor, so that through his poverty you might become rich" (*2 Cor 8: 9*).[4] The Son of God became poor by assuming our mortal flesh. But that was not all: he chose to be poor among men; he counted himself among the *anawim*, the "poor ones" of Jahweh. His parents were poor, Bethlehem and Nazareth were poor villages. During his public ministry he had "nowhere to lay his head" (*Mt 8: 20*). He preached his gospel to the poor and he died poor, stripped of everything, on the cross.

We saw his glory

God became man. He became an infant. What could be more helpless than an infant, completely dependent on its mother? It is this aspect of Christmas which appeals so strongly to religious sentiment. Popular devotion is drawn as by a magnet to the child in the manger, with the young mother kneeling at his side and St Joseph standing guard. It is a scene of tenderness which has inspired countless carols and has been depicted so many times in paintings and sculpture.

It would be wrong to disparage this very human approach to the mystery even if some of its expressions, in Christmas cards for example, are over-sentimental or even trivial. The liturgy is not insensitive to the human element, it, too, dwells with tenderness on the scene of Bethlehem. But this is always coupled with the theological view which sees the divine aspect of the mystery. Take,

for example, this antiphon for evening prayer of
28 December:

> The holy and undefiled virgin gave birth to God;
> when he took on the form of a helpless infant
> she fed him at her breasts; let us all adore him
> who has come to save us.

The note of tenderness is there: the helplessness
of the child and the maternal solicitude of Mary
draws our compassion. The predominant idea,
however, is that of the *greatness* of this child, who
in becoming man never ceases to be the Son of
God and whose mission in the world is to save all
people.

The divine and the human are maintained in
balance, sometimes contrasted in a kind of playful
antithesis, as in the verse of the fifth century hymn:
"A Mother's milk that strength renewed/which
gives the birds of heaven their food" (*parvoque
lacte pastus est / per quem nec ales esurit*). Here
the omnipotence of the divine nature is contrasted
with the lowliness of the assumed nature.

The overall impression left on us by the liturgy
is not that of the lowliness of the infant but of
his majesty. It extols the glory of the new-born.
It acclaims him as Lord and King. This is very
noticeable in the choice of psalms for the liturgy
of the hours, verses of which appear also as antiphons in the Office and Mass. These psalms are
chosen by design from that group within the
psalter which include the messianic and royal
psalms, and the psalms of enthronement. Psalm 2,
which begins the Office of Readings on Christmas

Day, is a good example since it has always formed part of the festal liturgy in Jerusalem as well as in Rome. It extols the kingship of Christ: "It is I who have set up my King on Sion, my holy mountain"; also his divine origin: "The Lord said to me; 'You are my Son, it is I who have begotten you this day'".

In the course of Christmas and Epiphany we shall hear much of the glory of the new-born king. It could be described as a liturgy of glory. This is not an exaggeration since the gospels also present Jesus in this light. St John, who declares that the "Word was made flesh", also tells us that "we saw his glory". The other evangelists and St Paul have the same message.

"For there is a child born for us, a son given for us . . ." These words from Isaiah we hear in the first reading *(Is 9: 1-7)* at the midnight Mass. They remind us that this child was in outward appearance no different from any other child; he was born under conditions less favourable than those of other children. And yet our faith tells us that this child is the Son of God. This prepares us for what the prophet then goes on to say: "and this is the name they give him, Wonder-Counsellor, Mighty-God, Eternal-Father, Prince-of-Peace".

God's love revealed

Let us consider that passage from *Hebrews* read at the third Mass for Christmas day: "In many and various ways God spoke of old to our fathers by the prophets; but in these last days he has spoken to us by a Son" *(Heb 1: 1-12)*. In a similar vein St John concludes the prologue to his gospel with the words: "No one has ever seen God; it is the only Son, who is nearest to the Father's heart, who has made him known" *(Jn 1: 18)*.

The Old Testament is the history of God's revelation. In it we see how God communicated with his people, how he led them stage by stage to a fuller knowledge of himself, how he unfolded his great plan for the salvation of his people and of the world. He spoke to his people through the events of their history and especially through the prophets who were his chosen messengers and interpreters. One of these prophets, Isaiah, was our constant companion during Advent and he is heard again at Christmas.

Then in the fulness of time God sent his Son into the world, "born of a woman, born under the law" *(Gal 4: 4)*. He speaks to us no longer through messengers but through a Son, his only-begotten Son. He is, in the expression of St John, the *Word* of God. He is the Word who, in human form, makes known to us who the Father is. He is the "radiant light of God's glory and the perfect copy of his nature" *(Heb 1: 3)*, He is the revelation of God's love.

Christmas should be a time of prayerful listening to that Word. God speaks to us at all times, but with special power in this season. He is speaking to us and we must listen with heightened attention. He addresses us through his beloved Son in whom he is well-pleased.

To receive this word, to be open and responsive to it, requires an effort on our part. It calls for attentiveness and silence; not just external silence but, more important, the inner silence of our imaginations, our thoughts and preoccupations. We must try to create a zone of silence within ourselves where the voice of God — a "still small voice" — can be heard.

The silence of Christmas! The entrance antiphon for the second Sunday after Christmas evokes the atmosphere of that first coming in words taken from the Book of Wisdom: "When peaceful silence lay over all, and the night had run half of her swift course, your all-powerful word, O Lord, leaped down from heaven, from the royal throne" *(Wis 18: 14-15)*. St Ignatius of Antioch seems to have this text in mind when he speaks of the "one sole God who has revealed himself in his Son Jesus Christ, *Word of his own from silence proceeding*".[5]

The message of Christmas is, in a sense, an unspoken one. In the infancy narrative as described by Luke, there is again this atmosphere of silence. There is much movement but few words. The child in the manger cannot speak. He has to grow up and learn like every other child. Of Joseph, his foster father, no single word is recorded. Mary his mother says little but ponders over all these things "in her heart" *(Lk 2: 19)*.

But the events speak for themselves, they require no commentary. They are more eloquent than any amount of words. They speak to us of the immensity of God's love. And so, with the shepherds, "let us go to Bethlehem and see this thing (*rema*, a word or happening) which the Lord has made known to us" *(2: 15)*.

The apostles John and Paul each speak of the revelation of God's love in Christ. The evangelist says: "God's love for us was revealed when God sent into the world his only Son, so that we could have life through him" (*1 Jn 4: 9;* midday office of Christmas); and his thought finds an echo in preface II: "Today you fill our hearts with joy as we recognise in Christ the revelation of your love". St Paul explains the motive and the effects of this love in the second reading of the dawn Mass *(Titus 3: 4-7):*

> When the kindness and love of God our saviour for mankind were revealed, it was not because he was concerned with any righteous actions we might have done ourselves; it was for no reason except his own compassion that he saved us . . .

The loving kindness of God! This renders the Latin word, *humanitas* (humanity), which translates the Greek *philantropia* (literally "love for man"). Kindness, compassion, generosity — these are words Paul uses as attributes of our God who has become more fully known to us in the incarnation.

In the Old Testament, too, God gave many proofs of his love. He was not only the God of justice, as is sometimes claimed. But he was not fully known. To some devout souls he was indeed known as the Father of Israel and the God of tender compassion, but among the people at large he tended to be the God of tremendous majesty. Fear played a large part in Old Testament piety.

In one of his Christmas sermons, St Bernard contrasts the revelation of God's love in the New Testament with that of his power and majesty in the old:[6]

> The kindness and humanity of God our Saviour appeared. Before his humanity appeared, his kindness lay concealed. What greater proof could he have given of his mercy than by taking upon himself that which needed mercy? Where is there such fulness of loving-kindness as in the fact that the Word of God became perishable like the grass for our sakes? The lesser he has made himself in his humanity, the greater he has shown himself in kindness. The more he humbles himself on my account, the more powerfully he engages my love.

In that conclusion lies another aspect of Christmas. God's love must be reciprocated. In preface I we declare: "In him (Christ) we see our God made visible and so are caught up in love of the God we cannot see". In Christ the gulf separating God and his creatures has been bridged. God has drawn near to man and has become more lovable.

The realisation that we are so loved by God should move us to love others. It is in truth the same love with which we love our Creator and our fellow-creatures. We should imitate God's loving-kindness, the divine *philantropia*. What we call the Christmas spirit, that attitude of generous good-nature which overcomes people at this time, is indeed a reflection of that love for mankind manifested in the incarnation. Let us not be satisfied with anything less than the true Christian spirit. Mere sentiment is not enough. In the people I encounter, especially the less fortunate of them, I must recognise the object of God's love and serve Christ in them.

A Saviour is born

The angels announced to the shepherds: "Today in the town of David a Saviour has been born to you" *(Lk 2: 11)*. From the moment of his appearance on earth, his role and mission is proclaimed. How frequently in the Christmas liturgy the title "Saviour" is applied to Christ, and the word "salvation" to his work!

Christmas and Easter, these two poles of the liturgical year, are not unrelated. There is, in fact, a close affinity between them. The Church fathers were aware of this, as were spiritual men and women of every age. In our own time, the following lines were written by Dag Hammarskjold on Christmas eve, 1960: "For him who looks towards the future, the manger is situated on Golgotha, and the cross has already been raised in Bethlehem".

For the fathers of the Church, with their unified vision of the mysteries of Christ, the work of redemption was initiated and partly realised in the incarnation and nativity. They held firmly, of course, that mankind was saved by Christ's sacrifice on the cross. At the same time, they did not dissociate his coming on earth from the redemptive work as a whole which culminated in the paschal mystery. For them the incarnation was a *saving mystery*. It was not only the beginning of salvation and the necessary condition for its accomplishment, but was itself "pregnant with the mystery of salvation".[7]

The explanation of this view lies in the fact that the Son of God in becoming man thereby elevated and ennobled human nature as a whole. By virtue of his incarnation, Christ draws to himself all humanity and leads it back to its first perfection.

By way of illustration, let us return to the three Christmas Masses. Notice how the second reading sets before us the whole redemptive work of Christ. These texts are *Titus 2: 11-14* (midnight Mass), *Titus 3: 4-7* (dawn Mass) and *Hebrews 1: 1-6* (day Mass). Here we find phrases such as: "He sacrificed himself for us"; "he saved us by means of the cleansing water of rebirth and by renewing us with the Holy Spirit"; "and now that he has destroyed the defilement of sin, he has gone to take his place in heaven at the right hand of the divine majesty". Here our attention is drawn to the cross by which our salvation was wrought; Also we are reminded of Christ's redeeming activity which continues in heaven through his intercession with the Father and on earth through the sacraments.

In the readings from *Ephesians* and *Collosians* during the days of the octave one finds the same comprehensive view of God's plan, centred in the passion, death, and resurrection of Christ.

In conclusion, we may cite other texts from the liturgy which illustrate the above theme. In a responsory for Christmas day the following is said: "A day of new redemption has dawned, a day of eternal bliss, prepared from of old". In the prayers, too, the redemption is frequently evoked, as for example, in the concluding prayer for the feast: "We welcome him with joy as our redeemer; year by year renew that joy as we await the fulfilment of our redemption". In another prayer from the dawn Mass we find this petition: "Accept our gifts on this joyful feast of our salvation".

The purpose of Christ's coming into the world is not just to teach and be a light to men, but to redeem mankind. His full mission is stated in the second Christmas preface: "He has come to lift up all things to himself, to restore unity to creation, and to lead mankind from exile into your heavenly kingdom".

In the light of these and other texts, we begin to see Christmas in its relationship to Easter, the great feast of redemption. It points to the latter and is fulfilled in the latter. It contains the element of sacrifice, for Christ coming into the world declares: "God, here I am! I am coming to obey your will" *(Heb 10: 7)*. This sacrificial note need not detract from the joy of the feast. It simply completes it. It reminds us that our commemoration does not stop short at the birth and infancy of Jesus, but embraces his whole life-span from the cradle to the cross and beyond, and that, in the words already quoted "the cross has been raised in Bethlehem".

The wonderful exchange

One of the great themes of Christmas is that of the "wonderful exchange". The Son of God, becoming incarnate, bestows on us a share in his divinity. The incarnation is a mystery shared. This leads us into the theology of grace.

In the office of readings for Christmas day, Pope St Leo exhorts us thus: "Sharers now in the birth of Christ, let us break with the deeds of the flesh. O Christian, be aware of your nobility — *it is God's own nature that you share*". The pope is here applying the moral teaching of St Peter who declares that we have become "partakers of the divine nature" *(2 Pet 1: 3-4)*.

This sharing in the divine nature is something already acquired and it is, at the same time, a reality which may grow and develop. In the concluding prayer of the feast we ask that this "wonderful exchange" may be perfected in us:

God our Father,
our human nature is the wonderful work of your hands,
made still more wonderful by your work of redemption.
Your Son took to himself our manhood,
grant us a share in the godhead of Jesus Christ.

This may remind us of another short prayer which we hear at the presentation of gifts in the

Mass. As the priest adds the drop of water to the wine in the chalice, he says: "By the mystery of this water and wine, may we come to share in the divinity of Christ, who humbled himself to share in our humanity". This formula derives from the Christmas oration quoted above. The latter has been slightly adapted to give it a marked eucharistic emphasis but the idea is the same.[8]

What is begun in baptism, this sharing in the divine nature, is progressively strengthened and deepened by the eucharist. This thought is suggested by the prayer over the gifts and the prayer after communion of the midnight Mass. In the first it is asked, "By our communion with God made man, may we become more like him who joins our lives to yours": and in the second, "may we share his life completely by living as he has taught". It is an idea we meet from time to time in the postcommunion prayers.[9]

This mysterious transaction whereby God takes what is ours and bestows what is his is beautifully evoked in the first antiphon for evening prayer on the octave day of Christmas:

> O wonderful exchange (O admirabile commercium)! The Creator of human nature took on a human body and was born of the Virgin. He became man without having a human father (sine semine), and has bestowed on us his divine nature.

So real is this sharing in the divine nature that the Church fathers could speak of man's "deification" through grace. We associate this idea especially with the Greek fathers, but it is also to be met with among Western theologians, notably in the writings of St Augustine.[10] This doctrine is summed up in the aphorism: "God became man in order that man might become God". It is a strong affirmation which stresses the reality of grace without however removing the distinction between the Creator and the creature.

In a reading for 30 December, St Hippolytus explains how the Word made flesh deifies us. He says: "All that belongs to God, he has promised to give you, because you have been deified and have become immortal". He concludes with the words: "God is not lacking in anything, and he made you also a god for his glory". Pope St Leo affirms the same truth in a more qualified way (reading for 31 December). He declares that the Saviour "became the Son of man in order that we might have the power to be the sons of God".

It is through union with the Son that we become sharers in the divine nature. Through that union we are introduced into the intimate life of Father, Son, and Holy Spirit. Our deification is the consequence of our divine adoption. What Christ is by nature, the Son of God, we become by grace. Through our incorporation with him, we are made "sons in the Son" (filii in filio), to use the expression of Fr Emile Mersch.[11]

The mystery of our divine adoption, which becomes a reality for each one in baptism, has its origin in the Incarnation. The midnight Mass at Christmas begins with the words of the entrance antiphon: "The Lord said to me: You are my Son;

this day have I begotten you" *(Psalm 2: 7)*. In their liturgical context, these words are spoken by the eternal Father to his Son. They speak of Christ's divine origin, before time began, and of his birth at a moment of history. These words are also addressed to us, because in the Father's plan we are not separated from the beloved Son. In his incarnate Son, God the Father recognises us and embraces us as his children.

The realisation in prayer that we are indeed the children of God is surely one of the cherished graces of Christmas. For some favoured souls this was an abiding intuition, Abbot Columba Marmion realised it with all his being. St Theresa of Lisieux understood and lived this doctrine in her little way of spiritual childhood. It must become a reality for us as well.

If God deigns to address us as his children, then we dare to call him Father. Indeed, we dare to call him by the more personal and intimate name of "Abba". St Paul learned this in prayer and he shares his experience with us: "The proof that you are sons is that God has sent the Spirit of his Son into our hearts: the Spirit that cries, 'Abba, Father', and it is this that makes you a son, you are not a slave any more" (from *Galatians 4: 4-7*, the second reading for the octave day of Christmas).

Since we share all the mysteries of Christ, his birthday is also ours. His birth of the Virgin Mary is for us the "beginning of new life", and in celebrating this feast we are commemorating our own "sacred beginnings". This is the thought of Pope

St Leo, to whom we give the last word on the meaning of Christmas:

> As we adore the birth of our Saviour we find that we are celebrating our own beginnings *(sacra primordia)*. For the birth of Christ is the origin of the people of Christ, and the birthday of the head is the birthday of the body.[12]

7 Solemnity of Mary, Mother of God

Today is the octave of Christmas and the first day of the new year, a conclusion and a beginning. The Church dedicates it to her who has been called the "Virgin of the way", whom we meet at every stage of life's journey, at its inception and "at the hour of our death".

In the new, revised liturgical Calendar it has been given its present title. The designation makes it clear that this is a feast of our Lady and that its object is to honour with fitting solemnity her divine maternity. Before its change of title in 1969 the feast was known as the "Circumcision of our Lord". This too is commemorated, as is the giving of the name Jesus to Mary's child, but the principal object of the feast is the virginal motherhood of Mary, contemplated in the light of Christmas.

Actually, the liturgy of this day always had a distinctly Marian character, so that the change of title amounts to little more than a making explicit what was implicit in the Mass and office of the octave of Christmas. Historians of the liturgy have for long been aware that this feast of 1 January is, surprisingly enough, the oldest celebration in honour of our Lady in the Roman liturgy.[1]

The antiphons, which exalt the divine maternity of Mary, are taken from the old office and have been in use for many centuries. Here is one beautiful example from morning prayer:

Mary gave birth to the king whose name is eternal; she united the joy of a mother with the honour of a virgin; such as this has never happened before nor will happen again, alleluia.

The title *Theotakos* (God-bearer) was applied to Mary by the Greek fathers from as early as the third century. This title was upheld by the Councils of Ephesus and Chalcedon. In the West she was likewise honoured as *Dei Genetrix* (Mother of God). In the ancient Roman canon she is commemorated as "the ever-virgin mother of Jesus Christ our Lord and God".

In the words of Pope Paul VI: "The Christmas season is a prolonged commemoration of the divine, virginal and salvific motherhood of her whose inviolate virginity brought the Saviour into the world". Today's feast is a summing up and a highlighting of this mystery. It is meant to "exalt the singular dignity which this mystery brings to the holy Mother through whom we were found worthy to receive the Author of Life".[2]

In addition to Mary's role as "God-bearer", there is her spiritual maternity with regard to mankind. Just as Eve was the "mother of all the living" in the natural order, Mary is Mother of all the living in the order of grace. For in giving birth to her first-born, she also gave birth spiritually to those who would belong to him, who would be incorporated with him and so become his members. He is the "first-born of many brethren", the Head of redeemed humanity, the representative of mankind who unites all things in himself.

In the new liturgy we note a concern to bring out more clearly the relationship between Mary and the Church. In today's feast there is in the postcommunion prayer an explicit reference to Mary's maternal role with regard to the people of God: "Father, as we proclaim the Virgin Mary to be mother of Christ and mother of the Church, may our communion with her Son bring us to salvation". This shows that she is the mother of the Head and of the members, the "holy Mother of God and therefore the provident Mother of the Church".[3]

In Mary's own life there was a growing consciousness of her spiritual maternity. Even at the annunciation she would have had a presentiment of her role as mother of the Messiah. She knew that God had great designs for her Son and this would involve her in renunciation and suffering on behalf of his people. She would be giving birth to a saviour of his people, a man for others. Her role would be entirely subordinate to his. She implicitly accepted her share in his mission, and, as the destiny of her Son unfolded itself, she continued to re-affirm her assent. So it was when she presented her first-born in the Temple; she renounced all claims over her child and offered him to God and to his people. This spiritual maternity reached its high point at the foot of the cross, and then it entered a new phase at Pentecost.

The Virgin Mary continues her maternal role in heaven: "For, taken up to heaven, she did not lay aside this saving role, but by her manifold acts of intercession continues to win for us gifts of eternal salvation".[4] That is why the faithful, from very early times, have invoked her as Mother — *mater Christi, mater gratiae et misericordiae* — and now *mater ecclesiae*, mother of the Church. This reliance on the prayers of the Mother of Jesus is not just pious sentiment but rather the effect of a deep conviction that she has a mother's love and solicitude for all Christ's brethren and that her prayers have an efficacy greater than that of any other saint. In the words of one theologian: "Mary, in her glorified state in heaven, must always remain a mystery of intercession and of maternal mediation".[5]

Not only is the feast of 1 January the oldest Marian feast in the Roman liturgy, it also has exceptional importance and merits the prominence it has now been given. For the mystery of the divine maternity is really the fundamental truth about the Virgin Mary. Other feasts rank higher, but it must be remembered that the two most important of these have a direct bearing on today's feast. The Immaculate Conception has in view of Mary's role as Mother of the Incarnate Word. It was the means God chose to prepare a worthy dwelling place for his Son. The greatest of Mary's feasts, the Assumption, is but the consequence of her divine motherhood, for it was not fitting that the "Tabernacle of God" should suffer corruption.

The doctrine of the divine maternity is not only

a Catholic dogma, it is a belief we share with many Christians of other denominations as well. This is significant since, generally speaking, Protestants have difficulty with the Immaculate Conception and even with Mary's Assumption into heaven. Here at least we are on common ground for, as one of their own spokesmen has said: "When you say that Mary is the Mother of God, you have said everything".[6]

In one of the Latin hymns to our Lady there is the verse *Monstra te esse matrem,* "Show yourself to be truly a mother to us". It is not enough to believe in her intercessory role, we must experience it too. We should have an abiding sense of her presence in our lives, near to her Son and near to us. This is the secret of Catholic devotion to our Lady, and it is the grace asked for in the concluding prayer of the feast, "Grant that we may feel the power of her intercession when she pleads for us with Jesus Christ your Son, the author of life".

World Day of Peace

Pope Paul VI has made this a special day of prayer for universal peace. Having spoken of its liturigical singificance as octave of Christmas and solemnity of the Mother of God, he goes on to say:

> It is likewise a fitting occasion for renewing adoration to the newborn Prince of Peace, for listening once more to the glad tidings of the angels; and for imploring from God, through the Queen of Peace, the supreme gift of peace.

It is for this reason that, in the happy concurrence of the octave of Christmas and the first day of the year, we have instituted the World Day of Peace, an occasion that is gaining increasing support and already bringing forth fruits of peace in the hearts of many.[7]

The whole message of Christmas could be summed up in the word "peace", and it is this peace which the Church tries to bring to the world. In the words of Pope St Leo, "The birthday of the Lord is the birthday of peace". He says that it is God's gift to us and also our gift to him, since there is nothing more pleasing to God than brothers living at peace with one another.[8]

The cynic might ask, "Has Christianity ever prevented wars? Has it not at times been at the centre of conflict?" It is true that Christ's coming on earth did not put an end to wars, nor has the Church been very effective in maintaining peace among nations. But in every age there have been great Christian leaders who have been heralds and instruments of God's peace in the world. The Church has always proclaimed peace, has sought to lead men into the ways of peace, and, in spite of disappointment and failure, she continues to "seek peace and pursue it".

The peace of Christ can exist even where there is war and sectarian strife. Christians, caught up in these conflicts, often bear witness to the peace of Christ which is in their hearts. They are ready, regardless of the cost, to forgive their enemies and to take the first step in being reconciled with their brothers. Christ did not promise us immunity from war. The peace which he bequeathed to us was one "the world cannot give" *(Jn 14: 27).*

Christian peace is not only of a spiritual kind. The Church has an obligation to promote peace among nations. She must be concerned about the welfare of all peoples. There can be no true and lasting peace where justice and human rights are denied. The popes of this century have all worked hard to secure peace for mankind. In the Christian view, peace is not just the absence of war, but a world order based on the recognition that all men are brothers and have a common Father in heaven.

8 Epiphany

Twelve days after Christmas the Church celebrates
Epiphany, a feast similar in character to the
preceding one. They are companion feasts, if not
identical twins. The name "Little Christmas" for
Epiphany expresses the popular understanding of
the feast in the Western Church. It appears as a
repetition, on a lesser scale, of the festivities of
Christmas. For Christians of the Eastern Church,
the reverse is true. They too celebrate Christmas,
but they do not accord it the same rank as Epiphany.
For them it might be appropriate to call the
feast of 25 December, "little Epiphany".

Whatever about the relative rank and importance
of these feasts, the truth is that the universal
Church celebrates both. Christmas and Epiphany
are complementary and mutually enriching feasts.
They both celebrate, from different perspectives,
the mystery of the Incarnation, the coming and
manifestation of Christ in the world. Christmas
places the accent on the coming, while Epiphany
emphasises the manifestation.

A look at origins

The Epiphany is of Eastern origin and was probably

first celebrated in Egypt. From there it spread to other Churches of the East and then moved westwards, first to Gaul and later to Rome and North Africa. The appearance of this feast in the early fourth century coincided approximately with the institution of Christmas at Rome. In the course of the century a process of mutual borrowing took place. While the Western Churches adopted the feast of Epiphany, those of the East, with some exceptions, were not long in introducing the feast of Christmas. As a result of this borrowing or "twinning", the Churches East and West were celebrating two great feasts at Christmas-time, and this as early as the fourth or fifth centuries.[1]

The feast of 6 January has been described as the Christmas of the Eastern Church. This would be a fair description if we are considering the period of origins. There is no doubt that at the time of its institution, the Epiphany commemorated the birth of Christ, and so was not so different from our Christmas; both were nativity feasts. It underwent a certain evolution, however, and this as a result of the influence of the Western Christmas. It seems likely that from the beginning it included at least one other theme, that of Christ's baptism in the Jordan. This theme gained in importance so as to become the primary object of the feast. The commemoration of the nativity was then reserved to Christmas.

The word itself, from the Greek *Epiphaneia* ("manifestation"), throws light on the original significance of the feast.[2] In classical Greek the word could express two ideas, one secular, the other religous. In secular usage it could refer to an *arrival.* When, for example, a king visited a city and made his solemn entry, that event was recorded as an *epiphany.* It is in this sense that St Paul uses the word with reference to Christ. His coming on earth was an epiphany, like that of a great monarch entering a town. Take, for example, this passage from *2 Timothy 1: 10:* "This grace had already been granted to us, in Christ Jesus, before the beginning of time, but it has only been revealed by the Appearing *(epiphaneia)* of our saviour Christ Jesus".[3] From this New Testament use of the word *epiphaneia,* it is easy to understand how the idea of nativity entered into the conception of the feast of Epiphany; for it celebrated the coming, the arrival, and the presence among us of the Incarnate Word.

Then there was the religious use of the term in Grecian culture. Here it had quite a different sense. It denoted any *manifestation of divine power on behalf of men.* Here we are closer to the liturgical understanding of Epiphany. It is a feast of mani-festation. God manifested his benevolent power at the Incarnation. Christ's coming on earth was itself an epiphany. Then there were other manifest-ations: the adoration of the Magi, the baptism in the Jordan, the changing of water into wine at Cana, and others as well.

It seems then that, from the beginning, the feast of Epiphany had a rather complex character. It was a feast of nativity, but it was also something more. It celebrated not just the historical coming on earth of our Lord and Saviour Jesus Christ, but also the various "signs" throughout his life by which he revealed his power and glory.

We have noted how, in the Eastern Church, the focus of interest tended to fix on the Baptism of Christ; not without reason, since it was then that the Father bore witness that this was his beloved Son and the Holy Spirit rested upon him in visible form. That was the manifestation which inaugurated his public ministry and revealed him as the Messiah.

With the introduction of the Epiphany to Rome and other Churches of the West, the significance of the feast also underwent a change. It was the episode of the Magi, following the star and coming with their gifts to worship the Messiah, which became the principal theme of the feast. A profound symbolism was attached to the gospel account. It represented the vocation of the Gentiles to the Church of Christ.

The call of the nations

When Epiphany comes round, it is customary to add the three figures of the Magi to the Christmas crib. They have certainly caught the popular fancy. Legend has given them names and made them into kings. In the great Gothic cathedral of Cologne you can see the shrine of the three kings. Their bones were brought there from Milan in 1164 by Frederick Barbarossa.

The great Latin fathers, St Augustine, St Leo, St Gregory and others, were also fascinated by these three figures; but for a different reason. They

were not curious to know who they were, where
they came from; nor were they interested in build-
ing legends about them. Their concern was to
determine what they *represented,* their symbolic
role, the theology underlying the gospel narrative.
And in their reflections on *Matthew 2: 1-12,* they
arrived at the same conclusions: the wise men from
the east represented the *nations of the world;* they
were the first-fruits of the Gentile nations coming
to pay homage to the Lord; they symbolised the
vocation of all men to the one Church of Christ.

In this interpretation of Epiphany, the feast
takes on a universal character. It widens our field
of vision, opens up new horizons. God no longer
manifests himself to a single race, a privileged
people, but to the whole world, the good news of
salvation is addressed to all men. The people of
God is now composed of men and women of every
tribe and nation and tongue. The human race constitutes a single family since God's love embraces
all.

This is the mystery which we, perhaps, take for
granted, but which St Paul never ceased to marvel
at. In the second reading of the Mass (*Eph 3: 2-6*),
he speaks of this mystery, hidden from past
generations but now revealed through the Spirit,
"that the pagans now share the same inheritance,
that they are parts of the same body, and that the
same promise has been made to them, in Christ
Jesus, through the gospel". Let us remember that
we too were once the "Gentiles". As St Peter reminded his pagan converts: "Once you were not a
people at all and now you are the People of God;

once you were outside the mercy and now you have been given mercy" (*1 Pet 2: 10*).

The vocation of the nations is the theme of St Leo's homily, read at the office of readings. He says: "In the three Magi let all the nations worship the Author of the universe; and let God be known, not in Judaea alone but throughout the whole world". Then an exhortation: "let us celebrate with spiritual joy the day of our first-fruits and the commencement of the nations". These wise men from the East represented the first-fruits (*primitiae*) of the great harvest of humanity. This is an idea which recurs in the patristic sermons for the Epiphany.

Towards the end of his homily St Leo introduces a missionary and evangelistic note. He observes that what the Church is celebrating is not just an event of long-ago, but a saving activity which still continues in the world. Wherever the gospel is preached and people are drawn to belief in Christ, there the mystery of the Epiphany is realised. This work of leading others to Christ is one in which we all share. All should be "at the service of this grace which invites all men to Christ".

In the first reading of the Mass, from *Isaiah 60: 1-6,* we have a splendid vision of the entry of the nations into the Church. The prophet foretells the return of the exiles to Jerusalem. The city is represented as a mother who mourned over the dispersal of her children and will soon rejoice at their return. In the liturgy this prophecy is seen fulfilled in the Church. She is also a mother and she rejoices to see her children coming from afar:

Lift up your eyes and look round;
all are assembling and coming towards you,
your sons from far away
and your daughters being tenderly carried.

A vision of universality, like a great procession of peoples from all parts of the world converging on the holy city, the Church. And these people come, not empty-handed but bearing gifts: "for the riches of the sea will flow to you and the wealth of the nations come to you". How are we to understand these gifts? Are they merely material wealth and resources or do they represent spiritual riches? I suggest that they are the latter, the invisible assets, and these include the inherited wisdom, the culture, and the religious traditions of each nation. All these must be drawn into the treasury of the Church, if she is to become fully catholic. Not everything can be assimilated. Some elements may need to be purified or even rejected, but the Church recognises that whatever values of truth and goodness are found among these peoples are signs of God's hidden presence among them. As the Council declares: "Whatever good is found to be sown in the hearts and minds of men, or in the rites and cultures peculiar to various peoples, is not lost".[4]

At this point we return to the three kings, for we seem to meet them in the responsorial psalm (*Ps 71*): "The kings of Tarshish and the sea coasts shall pay him tribute. The kings of Sheba and Seba shall bring him gifts". It may have been this psalm

which gave rise to the tradition, already found in
Tertullian, that the Magi were kings. Later the
gifts themselves were given a mystical interpretation. They signified divine mysteries. The gold
acknowledged Christ's regal power, incense his
high priesthood, and myrrh his passion and burial.

The guiding star

The next element in the story is the star which
guided the wise men to Bethlehem. We may pass
over in silence explanations concerning the nature of
the star. Some would identify it with a remarkable
conjunction of planets recorded in 7 − 6 BC, or
even with Halley's comet.[5] Such concern over de-
tails only leads to a neglect of the real point of
the story. The star is indeed an indispensable
element in St Matthew's account, but Christian
tradition interprets it not just as a natural phen-
omenon but as a *symbol of faith*.

The principal prayer of the feast, a prayer attrib-
uted to Pope St Gregory the Great, suggests this
latter approach. It is a prayer which links together
three ideas, the vocation of the nations, the star
as a symbol of faith, and the reward of faith which
is the face-to-face vision of God:

> On this day, Lord God,
> by a guiding star you revealed your only-begotten
>   Son
> to all the peoples of the world.
> Lead us from the faith by which we know you
>   now
> to the vision of your glory, face to face.

This prayer represents our own life as a pilgrimage, a pilgrimage of faith. We are the Magi. Faith is our guiding star. Bethlehem is our goal.

Faith is a light by which we recognise God. It is a star drawing us to Christ. It is a gift from God, an illumination, not something we possess of ourselves. Christ has said: "No one can come to me unless he is drawn by the Father who sent me" (*Jn 6: 44*). The light of revealed truth cannot be attained by human reason alone. It is God who reveals, it is he "who has shone in our minds to radiate the light of the knowledge of God's glory, the glory on the face of Christ" (*2 Cor 4: 6*).

Through faith we really *know* God, even if that knowledge is obscure, "as through a glass in a dark fashion". It is a knowledge which unites us to God and, even here on earth, brings with it the "guarantee" and the substance of things hoped for (see *Heb 11: 1*). We journey by faith, not by sight. We are like the air-pilot flying his plane by night. He sees nothing outside his cabin. Relying on his instruments, he knows that he is on the right course. Faith too sets us on our course, shows us the way forward.

At times we may lose our direction. The star, which appeared so bright, may grow dim and even disappear. That does no mean we are lost. This obscurity is temporary and serves as a testing of our faith. We should learn from the Magi. When they lost their star, they did not turn back. Instead, they sought advice from men versed in the scriptures who were able to tell them where the Christ would be born. We too should consult with those who, by their knowledge and experience, are in a position to help us. We need the advice of men and women who really know the word of God. To this must be added our own prayer and patience. Then the star will reappear . . .

The light of faith is something which can and ought to be shared. We need the witness of others and we in turn need to "bear witness to the light". The witness of a good life, of a faith that is lived, is far more telling than any amount of words. This is the message of the lighted candles at Easter and of the star at Epiphany. The light we have received must be communicated with our fellow-men. In the words of St Leo: "Whoever in the Church lives in piety and chastity, whoever is 'heavenly-minded, not earthly-minded', resembles this heavenly light; and while he preserves in himself the splendour of a holy life, like the star, he reveals to many the way to the Lord".[6]

But faith is not sight. It does not quench desire but inflames it. Man's ultimate happiness lies in the supernatural vision of God. We long to see him as he really is, to be led to the vision of his glory. This is the final goal, the ultimate reward, when the light of faith becomes the light of glory. This is something we dare hope for, since we have been promised "what eye has not seen, nor ear heard". On today's feast the Church asks for this greatest of gifts for all her children. Meanwhile we must be content with the light that we have, the light of faith which will "go on shining like a lamp in a dark room until the day breaks and the day-star rises in your hearts" (2 Pet 1, 19).

Secondary themes

The liturgy of Epiphany includes other themes or motifs which, if somewhat in the background, are important for our understanding of the feast. Traditionally, there are three manifestations which the Church commemorates and these are described in the Magnificat antiphon: "today the star led the Magi to the manger; today water was changed into wine at the marriage feast: today Christ desired to be baptized by John in the river Jordan to bring us salvation".

These are the three wonders (*tria miracula*). We have dealt with the first. Let us now consider the other two, beginning with the baptism of Jesus. As we have noted, in the Eastern liturgies this has become the principal theme of the feast. Not without reason, since the evangelists have attached so much importance to this mystery. All four mention it. St Mark begins his gospel with the preaching of John the Baptist and our Lord's baptism at his hands.

It was at his baptism that Jesus was manifested as the Son of God. It was then that the voice of the father was heard saying "This is my Son, the Beloved; my favour rests on him" *Mt 3: 17*). The Baptist, moved by the Spirit, also bore witness that this was "the lamb of God that takes away the sin of the world" (*Jn 1: 29*), thus announcing his saving mission. On the part of Jesus it was a humble act of submission whereby he ranked himself among the sinners. In doing so he bore witness to his love of the Father and of the people he had

come to save. This was the inauguration of his
public ministry and his solemn investiture as the
Messiah. The baptism also had prophetic significance. It announced another baptism, that of his
death on the cross, whereby he would finally
achieve our redemption, and it foretold the coming
of the Holy Spirit at Pentecost and the baptism
of all believers.[7]

It is surprising, considering the deep significance
of this event, that the baptism did not figure more
prominently in the Roman liturgy. Whatever
the reason, this neglect has now been made good. In
the days following the feast, all the various aspects
of the mystery are contemplated and commented
upon by the Church fathers in the patristic readings. What is more, the Sunday following the
Epiphany has now become the feast of the Baptism
of the Lord.

In celebrating the feast of our Lord's baptism
we are also commemorating our own baptism
and our adoption as God's children. When treating
of Christmas we considered how the mystery of
our divine adoption began at the Incarnation. On
today's feast we are reminded that it was on the
day of our baptism that our adoption became a reality for each one of us. The liturgy recalls this gift of
God and also reminds us of our obligation to live
as children of God. In one of the petitions we ask:
"Your baptism has made us children of the Father;
grant the spirit of sonship to all who seek you".
And in the concluding prayer, addressing the
Father, we say: "Grant that we, who by water
and the Holy Spirit are your adopted children, may

continue steadfast in your love".

The marriage feast of Cana is the third "wonder" commemorated in the Epiphany. It was the first sign that Jesus gave, the first manifestation of his divine power. In changing water into wine, "he let his glory be seen, and his disciples believed in him" (*Jn 2: 11*). Fr Joseph Lemarie, in his conclusion to a very full commentary on this episode, declares: "The miracle of the water changed into wine is the sign of the new dispensation which is the dispensation of the Spirit. By his Spirit, Christ transforms humanity and makes it pass from the state of sin and servitude to the glory and the liberty of adopted sonship. The two sources of this new life are baptism and the eucharist".[8]

The nuptial theme runs right through the Bible. The relationship of God and his people is that of husband and wife: "For your Maker is your husband", says Isaiah, "the Lord of hosts is his name" (*Is 54: 5*). It expresses God's faithful love for his people, and the symbol of that love is the covenant. The Creator and his creatures are bound together by this covenant which is like a marriage pact.

Then came the new dispensation: "God loved the world so much that he gave his only Son" (*Jn 3: 16*). The Incarnation was the consummation of God's union with men. That is why the Church fathers liked to present the mystery of the Incarnation as a kind of mystical marriage. St Gregory the Great, in a homily on the parable of the wedding feast (*Mt 22: 1-14*), explains how God the Father prepared a marriage feast for his Son when he united his nature to ours in the chaste womb of the Virgin Mary (Homily 38 of the Gospels). The image is well suited to express the divine charity which motivated the Incarnation. We have met it in the Christmas liturgy, especially in the antiphons and psalms. One example is the Magnificat antiphon for Christmas day: "He comes forth from the Father like a bride-groom coming in splendour from his wedding chamber".

In the New Testament the title of Bridegroom is applied to Christ. His bride is the Church. His coming on earth, the years of his hidden life and of his public ministry, have the joyful character of a wedding celebration. He forbade his disciples to mourn while the bridegroom was still with them (*Mt 9: 15*). John the Baptist was proud to be the "friend of the bridegroom", his apostles were his attendants, and all were his invited guests.

The marriage feast of Cana provides a joyful conclusion to the Christmas season. It expresses in graphic form the super-abundance of life, the "new wine" which Christ dispenses to his bride, the Church. It seems to knit together all the various threads of the Christmastide liturgy, and is admirably summed up in the antiphon for morning prayer on the feast of the Epiphany:

Today the Church has been joined to her heavenly bridegroom, since Christ has purified her of her sins in the river Jordan: the Magi hasten to the royal wedding and offer gifts; the wedding guests rejoice since Christ has changed water into wine, alleluia.

Notes

1   Advent — a new beginning

1.   *Mediator Dei,* chapter 2, no. 28.
2.   *Divine Office* 1, Wednesday of week 2, p. 30 and Thursday of week 2, p. 35.
3.   From a pastoral letter: Office of Readings for Monday, Week 1 of Advent, p.54.
4.   From his discourse on Psalm 118: *Divine Office* 111, pp. 286-88.
5.   Office of Readings, Wednesday of 1st week of Advent, p. 61.
6.   From the *Catecheses,* 15: 1-3, p. 49 of Breviary.
7.   See "Day of the Lord" in *Dictionary of Biblical Theology,* edited by X. Léon-Dufour (London, Chapman, 1967).
8.   *The Eternal Year,* p. 16.

2   Season of Hope

1.   See reading from Constitution on the Church, Tuesday of 2nd week of Advent, Breviary p. 81.
2.   Pastoral Constitution on the Church in the Modern World, no. 45.
3.   *The Church in the Modern World,* no. 43; see also nos. 21 and 39.
4.   *Parochial and Plain Sermons,* IV, pp. 322-25. Quoted by C. S. Dessain in *Newman's Spiritual Themes* (Dublin, Veritas, 1977), pp. 136-7.
5.   From ch. 1 of the *Proslogion;* p. 68 of the Breviary.
6.   Sermon 147, p. 89 of the Breviary.
7.   Reading for Friday of 3rd week from discourse on Psalm 37; Breviary, pp. 115-7.
8.   *Acta Apostolicae Sedis,* 31 May 1977, p. 285.

9.   *The Shaking of the Foundations* (Penguin, 1969), pp. 151-4.
10.   Breviary, p. 44.
11.   Breviary, p. 40.
12.   Breviary, p. 40.
13.   Sunday of first week, Breviary p. 5.
14.   Sunday of second week, Breviary p. 5.
15.   Friday of second week, Breviary p. 40.

3   Our Lady in Advent

1.   Nos. 53 and 56.
2.   Homily 4: 8-9, *In Praise of the Virgin Mother,* Office of Readings for 20 December, pp. 141-2.
3.   *Against the Heresies,* pp. 91-2 of Breviary.
4.   Sermon 25: 7-8.
5.   Constitution on the Sacred Liturgy, no. 103.
6.   Constitution on the Church, no. 68.

4   Rejoice in the Lord

1.   Now placed as second reading for year C.
2.   *The Mass through the Year,* Vol. 1, p. 15 f.
3.   *Isaiah* 2: 1-5; 9: 1-6; 11: 1-9; 28: 16-17.
4.   P. Jounel, "Les origines de l'Avent liturgique" in *L'Eglise en Prière,* ed. by A. Martimort, pp. 754-57.
5.   From 4 *Esdras,* Ch. 16; an apocryphal writing.
6.   *Meditations and Devotions* (London, Longmans, 1935), pp. 1-2 of "Meditations on Christian Doctrine".
7.   *L'Eglise en Prière,* p. 757
8.   Breviary, p. 149.

5   Christmas through the ages

1.   See J. Jungmann, *The Early Liturgy* (London, Darton, Longman and Todd, 1960), pp. 147-49 and 266-77.

2. It was a Syrian monk, Dionysius the Little, who in the 6th century devised our method of reckoning time by years BC and AD. Unintentionally, he placed the birth of Christ a few years too late. So according to our more accurate reckoning, Jesus was at least 5 years old in 1 AD.

6   The meaning of Christmas

1. Quoted by C. Dessain in *Newman's Spiritual Themes*, p. 58.
2. A. Nocent, *Célébrer Jésus-Christ*, Vol. 11, p. 45.
3. *Newman's Spiritual Themes*, p. 64.
4. Feast of the Holy Family, p. 203 of Breviary.
5. See *Divine Officer* 111, p. 331.
6. Breviary, p. 221 (abbreviated).
7. J. Lemarié, *La Manifestation du Seigneur* (Paris, Cerf, 1957), pp. 180-202.
8. J. Lemarié, *op. cit.*, p. 155.
9. See Missal, Common of Saints (3), Common of Bl. Virgin Mary at Christmas time, and 20th Sunday of year. Referred to by T. Krosnicki in *Ancient Patterns in Modern Prayer*, pp. 129-31.
10. See *The Theology of Grace* by C. Ernst (Cork, Mercier, 1974), p. 34 and pp. 47-52.
11. Cited by P. Fransen in *The New Life of Grace* (London, Chapman, 1969), p. 38.
12. Beviary, p. 243. The last line reads in Latin: *Generatio enim Christi origo est populi christiani, et natalis capitis natalis est corporis.*

7   Solemnity of Mary, Mother of God

1. Dom Bernard Botte drew attention to this in an article, "La première fête mariale de la liturgie

romaine" in *Ephemerides Liturgicae* 47 (1933), pp. 425-30.

2. Apostolic Exhortation, *Marialis Cultus*, no. 5.
3. *Marialis Cultus*, no. 11.
4. Constitution on the Church (*Lumen Gentium*), no. 62.
5. E. Schillebeeckx, *Mary, Mother of the Redemption* (Sheed & Ward, 1964), p. 129-30.
6. Quoted by one of the speakers at the 13th Glenstal Ecumenical Conference. The Protestant view is described by Rev. J. Haire in an article: "Born of the Virgin Mary", published in *Doctrine and Life* (August 1976) pp. 549-62. It was originally given as a lecture at this conference.
7. *Marialis Cultus*, no. 5.
8. Sermon 6 for the Nativity; Office of Readings for 31 December, p. 242 of Breviary.

8 Epiphany

1. For the historical background, consult J. Jungmann, *The Early Liturgy*, pp. 149-51; also Martimort, *L'Eglise en Prière*, pp. 746-53.
2. Here I follow C. Mohrmann, "Epiphania" in *Etudes sur le Latin de Chrétiens* (Rome, 1958), pp. 245-75.
3. See also 2 *Thess* 2: 8; 1 *Tim* 6: 14; 2 *Tim* 4: 1 and 8; *Tit* 2: 13.
4. Decree on the Missionary Activity of the Church, no. 9.
5. For whole scriptural background, see R. Brown, "The Meaning of the Magi; The Significance of the Star" in *Worship* 49 (Dec. 1975), pp. 574-82.
6. Sermon 23 for Epiphany.
7. See "Baptism" and sub-heading "Baptism of Jesus" in *Dictionary of Biblical Theology* (Léon-Dufour).
8. *La Manifestation du Seigneur*, p. 423.

Bibliography

Advent

BREEN, C., "Advent" in *Doctrine and Life* (November 1961).

CARMODY, J., "Advent Reflections" in *Bible Today* (December 1967), pp. 2309-14.

COLLECTIVE, a whole issue of *The Way* (October 1961) devoted to the Advent theme, "The Lord is nigh".

MERTON, T., "The Advent Mystery" in *Worship* (December 1963). pp. 17-24.

NOCENT, A., *Célébrer Jésus-Christ*, Vol. 1 (L'Avent); Paris, 1975.

ROGUET, A., *The Season of Hope* (Collegeville, Liturgical Press, 1961).

BLENKINSOPP, J., "The Coming of Christ" in *The Clergy Review* (December 1965), pp. 940-44.

Advent and Christmas seasons

ASHWORTH, H., "The Themes of the Patristic Liturgy: Advent, Christmas, Epiphany" in *Hallel* 3 (Advent 1975), pp. 235-66.

MAHER, M., "Advent and Christmas" in *The Furrow* (November 1976), pp. 597-605.

Scripture in Church, a periodical published by Dominican Publications, Dublin. Vol. 2, No. 4 and Vol. 3, No. 8 treat of the Scripture for Advent and Christmastide.

NOCENT, A., *Contempler sa gloire* (Paris, 1960).

The Feast of Christmas

BOROS, L., *Meditations* (these are meditations on Christmas), London, Search Press, 1973.

ETZWILER, L., "The Sacrament of Christmas" in *Doctrine and Life* (December 1962), pp. 613-20.

HARRINGTON, W., "The Nativity in St Luke" in *Doctrine and Life* (December 1963), pp. 618-22.

LEMARIE, J., *La Manifestation du Seigneur* (Paris, Cerf, 1957).

NOCENT, A., *Célébrer Jésus-Christ*, Vol. 2 (Noël-Epiphanie), Paris, 1975.

SPICQ, C., "Christ: God's love made manifest" in *Doctrine and Life* (December 1961), pp. 628-36.

COLLECTIVE, various scriptural and liturgical studies on Christmas in *The Bible Today* (December 1962).

Christology, grace, Our Lady

DESSAIN, C., *Newman's Spiritual Themes* (Dublin, Veritas, 1977), especially ch. 3, "Christ hidden".

LANE, D., *The Reality of Jesus* (an essay in Christology), (Dublin, Veritas, 1975).

KASPER, W., *Jesus, the Christ* (London, Burns & Oates, 1976).

ERNST, C., *The Theology of Grace* (Cork, Mercier, 1974).

FRANSEN, P., *The New Life of Grace* (London, Chapman, 1969) Apostolic Exhortation, *Marialis Cultus* (To Honour Mary) of Pope Paul VI. English edition published by Vatican Press, 1974; also in *Saints in Season*, edited by A. Flannery (Dominican Publications, 1976).

FLANAGAN, D., *In Praise of Mary* (Veritas, 1975).

SCHILLEBEECKX, E., *Mary, Mother of the Redemption* (Sheed & Ward, 1964).

After Christmas

BROWN, R., "The Meaning of the Magi; The Significance of the Star" in *Worship* 49 (December 1975), pp. 574-82.

O'DONNELL, J., *"The Purification"* in *Worship* 38 (January 1964), pp. 72-8.

BROWN, R., "The Presentation of Jesus (Luke 2: 22-40)" in *Worship* 51 (January 1977), pp. 2-10.